Outsmarting
Elderly
Embrace

"To outsmart elderly embrace is not to shun the wisdom of years gone by, but to intertwine it with the vibrancy of the present, crafting a tapestry of timeless grace."

DADHIRAM BASUMATARY
W: dadhirambasumatary.in

Foreword

Hey readers!

Isn't it fascinating that the true testament to love, commitment, and understanding is often not in the first blush of youth but in the later years of life? When two people have weathered countless storms together, celebrated numerous joys, and experienced life in all its varied hues?

That's the kind of love that "Outsmarting Elderly Embrace" celebrates. It's more than just a title; it's a celebration of lifelong companionship, the nuances of love that only become apparent with time, and the dance of two souls that have become so intertwined that their rhythms beat as one.

As the child of the authors, I've had the unique privilege of witnessing firsthand the kind of love and companionship this book embodies. It hasn't always been an easy journey - there have been challenges, disagreements, and times when the future seemed uncertain.

But through it all, the constancy of their love, their ability to embrace each other's imperfections, and their unending faith in each other's potential have been a beacon of hope for me and many others.

In "Outsmarting Elderly Embrace," my parents share the lessons they've learned, the moments that defined their relationship, and the secrets to struggling a loving bond in the autumn of life. Whether in the early stages of a relationship, in the throes of middle-aged love, or reflecting on decades of togetherness, this book offers a window into that kind of love that transcends time.

To my parents, thank you for inspiring me to write this book and live it. Your love story has been my guiding star, teaching me that love isn't just about the fiery passion of youth but also about the warm, gentle glow of the twilight years that promises to light up even the darkest nights.

I hope "Outsmarting Elderly Embrace" inspires, comforts, and reminds you that true love is timeless.

Warmest regards,

Dadhiram Basumatary

Introduction

Embracing Opportunities and Nurturing a Holistic Lifestyle

I am Dadhi Ram Basumatary, and the words you're about to read stem from my heart's deepest convictions. I see myself as a visionary, a warrior, and a guardian of our Earth.
I won't stand by and watch our world suffer. With every word I write and every speech I give, I aim to enlighten and inspire.

Every day, regardless of where I am – whether it's the open fields, academic halls, my writing space, or public platforms – I share a pressing message. My message isn't about giving up but about hope and acting.

I firmly believe that we have the power and the duty to stop the harm we're causing our planet. It's crucial for us to find a way to coexist with nature, valuing balance above all. It's truly an honor to stand before you today and share a piece of my journey.

I draw my inspiration from nature itself. Every sunrise and sunset renew my determination. The rustling leaves are not just sounds to me; they're voices joining mine, urging resistance against environmental crises and the harmful impacts of human actions.

As I stand before you today, feeling the weight of my journey in my heart, it's truly an honor to share the tapestry of my life's experiences.

I'm entirely dedicated to this cause, pouring my heart and soul into defending our planet. While I may not be a healer in the traditional sense, I contribute to Earth's healing in my own unique way.

As a fervent advocate for the tradition of Golden Peace Silk, I've come to realize the ethical richness it brings to the tapestry of our heritage. My journey with this tradition is a testament to resilience, determination, and the values we hold dear.

Please think of me as someone who plants seeds of ideas and dreams of a world where we live in harmony with nature. I am also a soldier, standing alongside many others, spanning nations and ages, in defense of our world.

I invite everyone to join me on this vital mission. We're on a journey to heal our mistakes and bring back the balance that ensures life flourishes. My words are not just about the challenges we face but also about hope and resilience.

My dedication motivates others to play their part in saving our planet. We're fortunate to have individuals like me, passionate and resolute, lighting the way to a sustainable and harmonious future."

Embracing the Full Spectrum of Life's Offerings and Pursuing a Harmonious Lifestyle. At its core, success is all about persistence and the unwavering belief that we can, and will, succeed."

"At the heart of true health lies the perfect balance between body, mind, and spirit." B.K.S. Iyengar.

Good day to each one of you! I trust you're feeling well. It's truly an honor to stand before you today and share a piece of my journey. I've always been inspired by the song "Try Everything," and it has taught me to grasp every chance that life presents, regardless of its shape or size.

My story starts with the simple life of farming. From there, I ventured into teaching, dove into the digital world as a trainer, and passionately advocated for solutions to global warming. Each of these roles has been a chapter in my ever-evolving tale of growth and exploration. Over the years, I've encountered some who have questioned my decision to donate 10–15% of my income to charitable causes. However, these acts of giving are a testament to my commitment to living a life that's not just about personal growth but also about giving back.

The essence of success lies not just in our talents but in the steadfast spirit of perseverance, and an unyielding belief in our visions.

In my quest for knowledge, intertwined with my profound love for nature, I've explored numerous fields of expertise. One significant area of my research centers around organic farming. I've delved deep into the potential of Trichoderma and mycorrhizae as vital components in promoting sustainable agriculture. The results have been promising, pointing towards a more environmentally friendly way of farming.

On another front, I'm passionate about promoting the use of peace silk. Recognizing the ethical and sustainable advantages it offers, I've been proactive in raising awareness about its significance. In this journey, I've also worked to address and resolve the unique challenges linked to its production.

Furthermore, my endeavors in beekeeping have been particularly enlightening. Through hands-on experience and research, I've discovered the intricate bond between effective beekeeping methods and the pollination success of local orchards. It's a relationship that underscores the balance and interconnectedness of nature.

Lastly but certainly not least, I've embarked on an ambitious project to rejuvenate over 1000 local orchid varieties. Leveraging traditional techniques of sapling multiplication, I'm determined to ensure these beautiful plants continue to grace our environment for generations to come."

As a writer and passionate advocate for the incredible tradition of Golden Peace Silk, my journey has taught me the power of resilience, determination, and ethical values. Embracing one's passions can be a challenging path, often laden with obstacles and demanding significant effort. Yet, these challenges should be seen not as setbacks but as motivations to propel us forward!

I am living proof that success is attainable through sheer determination and hard work. I'd like to debunk a common misconception: I don't possess any extraordinary talents that set me apart from others. What I do have is an unwavering commitment to my dreams. As the talented Shakira once sang, we should be willing to 'Try everything.' After all, it's through experimentation and persistence that we truly discover our potential."

Dear friends, I invite each of you to join me on a collective journey towards achieving our dreams. The road ahead promises a tapestry of incredible accomplishments waiting to be unveiled. Together, let's embark on this path, fueled by stories of unyielding spirit and tenacity. These narratives remind us that every single one of us holds the potential for greatness. It's all about having the right mindset and putting in the effort.

If you find yourself with only a handful of passions, do not be disheartened. Chasing what we love can indeed be a daunting task, requiring patience and persistence. Some may look at my journey and think I have been blessed with exceptional talents, unparalleled intelligence, or vast resources. But I am here to tell you that success doesn't hinge on any of these. At its core, success is all about persistence and the unwavering belief that we can, and will, succeed."

The shadows of my childhood were cast by the tumultuous relationship between my parents. My father's absences, marked by the haze of alcohol and bouts of anger, became the dark chapters of my early life. Yet, in those moments, the light of my sister's unwavering love guided me. If it wasn't for the unwavering love and support of my younger sister, I doubt I would have emerged strong from those trying times. I admit, for a while, I found solace in rice beer, but I've since moved past that phase. There were times I felt directionless, like an underachiever without a clear purpose. To cope, I took to farming and sought comfort in the company of friends, as both provided me with a respite from my tumultuous home life. The passing of my parents was a turning point in my life, marking my transition into a phase of growth and resilience.

Let me clarify further:

Despite their financial struggles and personal challenges, I am eternally grateful to my parents. Their lives, filled with adversity, provided me with invaluable lessons. The hurdles I encountered turned into steppingstones, shaping my character. But it's essential to understand that adversity and education alone won't mold you. Overcoming challenges, finding your true passion, and pursuing it with all your heart is what makes life worthwhile. The essence of life is love; without it, everything feels empty.

If you're seeking a fulfilling life and personal growth, it's vital to understand your innermost desires and recognize the barriers that hold you back. In my journey, I found a deep-seated passion for creating positive change. Academic credentials were imperative back then, leading me to pursue a degree in science.

Fast forward to 2020; the havoc caused by the coronavirus pandemic had lessened, but its aftershocks persisted. I started experiencing chronic fatigue and an overwhelming sense of unease. Fearing exposure to the virus or other illnesses, I avoided hospital visits. However, during a routine check-up, I was diagnosed with alarmingly high blood pressure. Though I've always been wary of allelopathic medicine, I had no choice but to start medication.

This health scare reminded me of a story from my past.

Back in 1916, due to a diet rich in carbohydrates and low in proteins and fats, my height is 176 CM, I weighed a hefty 96 kg, as per height should be 76 KG only, with a blood pressure of 160/100 mm Hg. Just like many of my peers, I was on daily blood pressure medication, a regimen I had to stick to for life. While I am not a fan of this necessity, it is vital for my health. Now, I'm researching natural ways to manage hypertension, with a primary focus on diet.

To aid in this quest, I've integrated regular yoga and jogging into my daily routine. Although results have been slow to come by, my determination to lose weight remains unwavering. Seeing my peers retire and some fall prey to terminal illnesses with no family history has only exacerbated my fears. The pain their families experienced was palpable, and I found myself questioning the reasons behind these tragic turns of fate. Regrettably, the medical world had only treatments for my symptoms, often through medicines or surgical interventions."

It's my time in the spotlight. A wise saying by Buddha goes, "What goes around comes around," and this resonates deeply with me. The year 2019 brought me a unique opportunity. I was chosen for a 15-day training in Modern Sericulture Processing Technology at Zhejiang Sci-Tech University in Hangzhou, China. The journey to this opportunity was far from straightforward, starting in Guwahati, India, passing through Kolkata, and finally landing in the mesmerizing city of Hangzhou.

Throughout the 17 days at Zhejiang Sci-Tech University, I met many fascinating individuals and ventured on exploration trips across various parts of China. One thing that particularly caught my eye was the noticeably small number of overweight people I came across. This observation led me to ponder the possible reasons.

A significant study from the early 1980s known as 'The China Study' holds some answers. This monumental research, a joint effort between Cornell University and the University of Oxford, delved deep into the relationship between diet and disease. China was selected for this research due to its broad regional diversity in disease occurrence. It also benefited from a backdrop of prior cancer research studies, setting the stage for an in-depth investigation.

With meticulous data collection across over 60 Chinese provinces and regions, the researchers analyzed the interplay between food habits and various health outcomes. They made extensive use of cancer atlases to decipher correlations between diet and illnesses such as cancer and heart disease. One startling revelation from their work was that eating meat posed a greater cancer risk than exposure to many known carcinogens. The research showed that reducing protein consumption, especially from animal sources, could markedly decrease cancer risks. This was further highlighted in a sub-study with rats: when exposed to the carcinogenic aflatoxin, rats on high-protein diets developed tumors nine times higher than their low-protein counterparts.

Yet not all proteins had the same effect. Rats consuming plant-based proteins like wheat or soy didn't show the same uptick in precancerous growths, hinting at the health benefits of plant-derived proteins. The China Study was instrumental in forging the connection between our dietary choices and disease risk, emphasizing particularly the potential hazards of high animal protein diets and the benefits of a plant-based approach.

Now is my moment to step into the limelight. A profound quote by Buddha asserts, "what goes around comes around." This sentiment deeply resonates with me. 2019 was a landmark year for me, presenting an opportunity I could have only dreamt of. I was selected for a 15-day specialized training on Modern Sericulture Processing Technology at the renowned Zhejiang Sci-Tech University in Hangzhou, China. The path to this prestigious training was a bit of an odyssey, starting from Guwahati in India, meandering through Kolkata, and culminating in the enchanting metropolis of Hangzhou.

During my 17-day stint at the university, I had the privilege of meeting a diverse array of individuals, each with their own unique story. I also took the opportunity to explore various regions of China, soaking in the culture, history, and natural beauty. One observation struck me profoundly: the remarkable fitness levels of much of the populace, with obesity seemingly rare. This stark contrast to many other parts of the world set me on a quest for understanding.

The answer, it seems, lay in a landmark study from the early 1980s, aptly titled 'The China Study'. A collaboration between Cornell University and the University of Oxford, this study undertook the Herculean task of understanding the diet-disease relationship. Given China's vast and diverse landscape, with varied dietary habits and patterns of disease prevalence, it was an ideal setting for such a study. The researchers built upon earlier cancer studies in the country, giving depth to their new venture.

The study spanned over 60 provinces and regions within China. The researchers meticulously collected data, aiming to understand the relationship between dietary patterns and health outcomes. Leveraging detailed cancer atlases, they sought correlations between specific diets and the prevalence of diseases such as cancer and heart disease. The results were eye-opening. A standout discovery was the heightened risk of cancer associated with high meat consumption — even more than many known carcinogens. The data suggested that a reduction in animal protein consumption could dramatically mitigate cancer risks. An auxiliary experiment with rats reinforced these findings. When exposed to aflatoxin, a known carcinogen, rats on a high-protein diet exhibited a much higher tumor rate than those on a low-protein diet.

However, the type of protein mattered. Rats fed plant-based proteins like wheat or soy showed no increased susceptibility to the precancerous changes, underscoring the potential health advantages of plant-derived proteins. 'The China Study' was pivotal in reshaping our understanding of diet and disease, especially shedding light on the hazards of animal-based proteins and endorsing the virtues of a plant-centric diet.

My Journey Through Trials and Triumphs

In 1987, my professional journey began with an oil company, which later became part of a renowned Navaratna firm in India. Those years could have been smoother; I faced numerous challenges, including discrimination in a supposedly progressive society. Still, I remained steadfast, focusing on my tasks, and brushing aside distractions.

A particularly challenging phase was when my wife was pregnant with our second child, Jabrang. A few days before her delivery, our company doctor, Dr. Dinesh Sarmah, suggested an x-ray to check for twins. Around that time, our daughter Jirina fell ill with tonsillitis. The recommended cure? Surgery.

I observed a personal health concern, too. My weight jumped from 74 kg to 96 kg. This change, I believe, was influenced by our diet—reminiscent of the American USDA food pyramid. We in India often lean towards high-carbohydrate meals and restrict fat and protein. I also faced health issues, deepening my reservations about conventional medicine, especially after developing an infection from a scooter accident.

Consequently, I looked elsewhere for healing. I found solace in homeopathy and connected with Subash Dev in Guwahati. That was my introduction to natural healing and wellness. While these might seem like mere episodes, they've profoundly shaped my faith in holistic health and guided me to a happier, healthier life.

Yet, my story could be more extraordinary. I wasn't an employee of the famed firm, but those years taught me one vital thing: my potential to help others. I realized I possessed insights that could be transformative. Over the years, these insights—small steps in lifestyle changes and tweaks in daily routines—have significantly improved my health and the lives of many.

From shifting diets—from paleo to Keto—to finally stabilizing at my goal weight and ideal blood pressure, every bit of progress resulted from small, consistent efforts. I've documented these in my upcoming book, "Holistic Weight Loss."

Starting in August 2024, I'll also offer personalized coaching for those keen on their wellness journey.

My Writing Odyssey

My writing adventure started in November 2022 with an article for dadhirambasumatary.com. Over the years, I've chronicled my experiments and findings on dietary practices. Though new to the publishing realm, my consistent writing habits—articles every other Sunday and Wednesday on Medium. com—earned me a significant following quickly.

Entering the writing world, I felt like an outsider. Yet, as months passed, I became recognized in the Eco-Holistic lifestyle domain. This tag brought both excitement and apprehension. My guiding light in this journey has been Padma Vibhushan <u>Dr. B.M. Hegde</u>, who believes in blending the best of Ayurveda, alternative medicine, and Western medical practices.

Why You Should Invest in This Book

In this book, I offer the wisdom I have accumulated over the years. From understanding which diets accelerated my healing post-injuries, to strengthening my mental and physical fortitude, to my evolution as a writer and entrepreneur, these tales reflect my transition to adulthood.

Your interest in this book likely stems from a desire for personal betterment. The "Eco-Holistic Outsmart to Obesity" series is designed to optimize your health and well-being. It advocates for balance—physical, mental, and spiritual. Among its myriad benefits, it'll guide you toward better nutrition, restorative sleep, and adequate exercise. By understanding the intricate links between your body, mind, and spirit, you'll be poised for personal growth and self-awareness.

"Why and How I Decided to Write This Series"

My first article for dadhirambasumatary.in was published in November 2022. Having documented my experiments with dietary habits for years, I felt compelled to share some of my insights with the public. Initially, I knew nothing about publishing; now, I publish new content at Medium.com every other Sunday and Wednesday, establishing a simple writing habit that garnered me my first thousand followers within months. As I embarked on this journey two years ago, I felt like an imposter. However, over time, I gained recognition in the Eco-Holistic lifestyle field, a new label that excited and troubled me. I approached this newfound status with a sense of unease. My role model has been Padma Vibhushan Dr. B.M. Hegde, a staunch advocate for combining Ayurveda and alternative medicine practices with Western medicine.

Rewards of Investing in This Book

In this book, I share the hard-earned wisdom I have acquired regarding how lifestyle choices can foster personal growth and happiness. I have learned that specific diets aided my recovery from injuries, enhanced my physical and mental strength, facilitated my journey as a successful writer and entrepreneur, and guided me toward responsible everyone. Your interest in this book suggests a desire to unlock your full potential. Reading the series "Eco-Holistic Lifestyle Approach" will yield numerous benefits, including improved overall health. By establishing a harmonious balance between body, mind, and spirit, a holistic fitness program aims to promote better mental health, alleviate depression, and equip you with practical tools to cope with stress, anxiety, and emotional turmoil. The book will guide you through optimizing your nutrition, enabling you to make healthier dietary choices that enhance your well-being. Additionally, it offers insights into improving sleep patterns, allowing you to awaken refreshed and ready to seize the day. Exercise in your holistic fitness routine can elevate your athletic performance and overall physical fitness. Embracing an eco-holistic approach to wellness engenders balance and fulfillment in all aspects of life, leading to heightened satisfaction and happiness. Moreover, reading this book will foster self-awareness, helping you understand the intricate connection between your body, mind, and spirit and how they impact your fitness and overall well-being. This newfound awareness will facilitate personal growth and self-realization.

Book Introduction:

Welcome to "Outsmarting Elderly Embrace": A Journey to Transform elderly Obesity." In this groundbreaking book, we explore the un know to western world fascinating connection between eco-holistic practices on health and wellness among the Asian adults. Through an engaging and evidence-based approach, we delve into the transformative power of aligning our lifestyles with the principles of nature, creating harmony within ourselves and the environment. By embracing eco-conscious choices, nurturing our bodies, and fostering a balanced mentality, we start on a path toward comprehensive, long-term weight reduction and improved health in all aspects of our lives. But to understand the true roots of the idea, we would have to go into its long and complicated past. One of the first systems of holistic (or "whole-body") medicine, Ayurveda dates back thousands of years. It is believed to have originated in India more than 3,000 years ago. The primary tenet of this school of thought is that physical, mental, and spiritual health are dependent on a harmonious coexistence amongst one another. Now This Ayurveda is Institutionalized to Ayush system in India under the <u>surveillance of WHO</u>. Do you imaging Ayurvedic practices still running in India kitchens, they use 50 -70 percent of Ayurvedic medicine as the spices in their daily dishes. Result everybody knows when Covid pandemic comes prediction of World altered and found Indians are more resilient, more immune resistant.

Here are some ground realities of the ancient Ayurvedic system:

· **Natural Healing:** The basis of <u>Ayurveda</u> lies in natural healing. It seeks to promote good health and wellbeing, not fight disease. But treatments may be recommended for specific health problems.

· **Three Doshas:** In Ayurveda, it's believed that everything in the universe, living or not, is connected. Good health is achieved when your mind, body, and spirit are in harmony with the universe. A disruption of this harmony can lead to poor health and illness. Ayurveda proposes that we are made up of a certain combination of the three doshas - Vata, Pitta, and Kapha. Any imbalance in these doshas leads to disease.

· **Preventive and Curative Aspects:** Ayurveda emphasizes prevention of disease, rejuvenation of our body systems, and extension of life span. It prescribes drugs, diet, exercise, and lifestyle recommendations to heal bodily diseases and mental illnesses.

· **Diet and Lifestyle:** The Ayurvedic diet is an integral part of the system. It doesn't follow a "one-size-fits-all" approach, and diet plans are individualized according to the patient's dosha balance. Ayurveda also emphasizes a healthy and balanced lifestyle.

· **Therapies and Treatments:** Ayurvedic therapies like Panchakarma cleanse the body, helping it get rid of accumulated toxins. Treatments are typically made from plants, but they may also contain metals, particularly in rasa shastra, the Ayurvedic practice of using metals in healing.

· **Scientific Validation:** While Ayurveda has been practiced for thousands of years and has been central to the health and wellness practices in India, some aspects of it are not scientifically validated in the same way as modern Western medicine. Studies have shown the effectiveness of Ayurveda in treating various diseases; however, some therapies need more extensive, rigorous scientific research.

· **Integration with Modern Medicine:** Today, Ayurveda is recognized as an alternative system of medicine and is being integrated with modern medicine in approaches like Ayurgenomics, a field marrying Ayurvedic principles with genomics.

So, the ground reality of the Ayurvedic system is that it's an ancient holistic healing system still in use today, both on its own and integrated with other medical approaches. It focuses on balance in the body's systems and uses diet, herbal treatment, and yogic breathing for maintaining and restoring that balance. Despite the lack of scientific evidence in some areas, many people find Ayurveda to be beneficial, and its practices are being explored more and more by the scientific community.

I'd be happy to share some lesser-known facts about the ancient Ayurvedic system:

· **1.** **Originated from Atharvaveda:** Ayurveda, which roughly translates to 'knowledge of life', is believed to have been derived from one of the four major texts of ancient Hindu philosophy, the Atharvaveda. It dates to about 5,000-10,000 years and is considered by some as the oldest healing science.

· **2. Three Doshas:** Ayurveda conceptualizes health in terms of balance among three elemental substances, or "doshas" - Vata (air & space), Pitta (fire & water), and Kapha (earth & water). Every person is considered to have a unique mix of these three doshas, and maintaining the balance between them is essential for health.

· **3. First Surgery Techniques:** Ancient Ayurvedic text, Sushruta Samhita, is known to describe the detailed surgical procedures, including types of surgical instruments, sutures, and postoperative care, making it one of the earliest comprehensive resources on surgery.

· **4. Health Holism:** Ayurveda doesn't just focus on the disease or symptomatic treatment but offers a holistic approach to health. It includes diet, lifestyle, mental and spiritual aspects, with a significant focus on prevention of diseases and maintaining health.

· **5.** **Panchakarma Detoxification:** Ayurveda incorporates a unique method of purification and rejuvenation known as Panchakarma. It's a combination of five procedures aimed at thoroughly cleansing the body of toxins.

· **6. Ayurveda and Mind:** Ayurveda holds that the mind plays a critical role in healing. Mental well-being is regarded as essential for physical health, hence practices such as meditation and yoga are often incorporated into Ayurvedic treatment plans.

· **7. Ayurvedic Pharmaceutics:** Ayurvedic texts describe the methods for drug preparation and treatment, including fermentation, distillation, and even therapeutic mineral and metal use, known as Rasa Shastra.

· **8. World's First Plastic Surgery:** The Sushruta Samhita is also known to describe what is essentially plastic surgery, including

rhinoplasty (the 'nose job') and otoplasty (earlobe reconstruction), which is quite a marvel considering the time when these procedures were developed.

· **9.Influence on Other Systems:** Ayurveda heavily influenced the development of traditional Chinese medicine and through it, some forms of western medicine. It also formed the foundation for Unani medicine and had a profound impact on Arabic and Persian medical systems.

· **10. Ayurveda and Longevity:** Ayurveda places great emphasis on longevity and advocates for a lifestyle that's in sync with nature's rhythm. It believes that by following an Ayurvedic lifestyle, one can achieve a long and healthy life.

These are just some of the many intriguing aspects of the ancient Ayurvedic system, and there's much more depth and richness to explore in its concepts and practices.

Chapter Titles and Outlines:

Introduction

Chapter 1:

How might Mother Nature's own remedies help soothe the wear and tear of our golden years?

Chapter 2

As our world evolves, how can the wisdom of eco-holistic health guide our footsteps to a heartwarming, ageless vitality?

Chapter 3:

In the quiet whisper of the trees and the gentle ripple of the brooks, how can we find secrets to rejuvenating our mature spirits?

Chapter 4:

How can embracing the beauty of nature enhance our well-being and paint our twilight years with colors of joy?

Chapter 5:

What ancient, earth-rooted practices can help the elderly feel more connected, grounded, and cherished in today's fast-paced world

Chapter 6:

As we look back at a lifetime of memories, how might the wonders of eco-holistic health help us craft a soul-nourishing journey ahead?

Chapter 7:

How does nature's embrace, through eco-holistic health, offer solace and strength to our aging hearts yearning for serenity?

Chapter 8:

As the sun sets on past chapters and dawns on new beginnings, how can eco-holistic approaches light our path towards holistic wellness?

Chapter 9:

What timeless lessons from the earth can help us age gracefully, embracing each moment with gratitude and grace?

Chapter 10:

How can the symphony of the natural world bring healing harmony to the challenges faced in our golden age?

Conclusion

Chapter 1:

How might Mother Nature's own remedies help soothe the wear and tear of our golden years?

The Golden Elixir

In a charming village situated between two mossy mountains, the locals faced an unusual issue in their old age. Despite having invaluable wisdom and experiences, they were plagued by numerous ailments that no modern medicine could alleviate. It was as if their golden years had lost their luster.

One of the village's oldest residents was Mrs. Neha, a graceful woman with silver hair and sparkling eyes. She felt that the village had changed, but the people had not. According to her, the solution to their problem lay in seeking answers from Nature.

A young and enthusiastic boy named Leo felt the same way. He decided to embark on a quest to discover Mother Nature's remedies for the elderly's ailments. With a notebook and an insatiable curiosity, he began his journey.

His first stop was the forest, where he met a wise old owl named Oren. Oren told Leo about the Gingko tree, whose leaves improved memory and concentration. They were a symbol of the forest's timelessness and, when brewed into a tea, brought clarity to aging minds.

Leo continued his journey to the top of a great mountain, where he met Tula, an ancient tortoise. Tula introduced him to a peculiar lichen growing on the mountain's rocks. Ground into a powder, it soothed aching joints and gave the elderly renewed strength.

Finally, Leo reached the ocean's edge, where he met Mira, a wise old dolphin. She told him about a particular seaweed that, when eaten, balanced energies and emotions, filling the elderly with joy and serenity.

With his notebook filled with knowledge, Leo returned to the village. The villagers combined all three remedies: Gingko tea every morning, a sprinkle of mountain lichen in the afternoon stew, and seaweed soup every night. As time passed, a transformation swept over the village.

The elderly, once bound by the constraints of age, danced at festivals. They told stories late into the night, their minds sharp and hearts light. Their golden years became genuinely golden, and the younger generation watched in awe, seeing for the first time the potential of a life lived to the fullest.

One day, Mrs. Neha took Leo's hand and said, "Nature has her ways, dear boy. We just needed to remember them."

The village thrived, and their golden years became a testament to the gentle power of Mother Nature's remedies, a beacon of hope for all who believed in the natural world's magic.

Nature's Embrace in the Golden Years: A Casual Dive into Timeless Remedies

Greetings readers! Today, I'd like to discuss the phase of life that we all aspire to reach - the golden years. As we age, our hair turns silver, and our pace slows down, but these years often reflect the stories we've written throughout our lives. However, the wear and tear of age and experience accompany these stories. The good news is that Mother Nature has always been ready to accompany us on this journey.

The art of life involves embracing the challenges and joys that every stage of life brings. As we enter our golden years, nature comes closer, offering remedies that can help us along the way.

Most of us have experienced a nagging backache or joint pain after a particularly strenuous day. That's where willow and turmeric come in - nature's very own aspirin, with the power to alleviate those aches. And as we grow older, who has yet to occasionally walk into a room and forget why? While I might joke about having a "senior moment," herbs like ginkgo biloba and rosemary stand by to bolster our memory.

Emotionally, our golden years can be a roller coaster. The changing dynamics of life can affect our moods. Here again, nature plays a therapist. St. John's Wort and the soothing scent of lavender can help balance our moods and soothe our spirits.

But what about the spirit itself, the very essence of who we are? As we age, we begin to appreciate the more profound, more tactile experiences of life. Have you ever walked barefoot on grass, feeling its cool embrace? Or touched the soft petals of a flower, marveling at its delicacy? These simple treasures become profound joys. Practices like shinrin-yoku or forest bathing, immerse us in the silent embrace of trees, grounding us in the present moment.

The golden years are not just about looking back at the life we've led. They are an invitation. It is an invitation to experience life deeply, to connect with our surroundings, and to embrace the wisdom that nature has to offer.

So, as we navigate the intricacies of aging, let's remember that we're not alone. With every step, sigh, and chuckle, nature is right there, offering her remedies, comfort, and boundless wisdom.

In our golden years, let's dance with nature, rejuvenate with her remedies, and cherish the wisdom of the ages. Because age is not just a number - it's a celebration. And nature? She's the life of the party.

Let's meander through this notion, much like one would stroll through an age-old forest, seeking out the elixirs that nature has always provided.

The Aches and Pains

It's funny how sometimes a question on a platform can bring back a flood of memories. Let me whisk you away on a little detour through my past. During my college years, I lived with my aunt in this Himalayan part of town, and she was a full-blown eco-holistic. Picture this: indoor plants everywhere, composting in the backyard, essential oils wafting through the air, and vegan diets.

One weekend, after a particularly indulgent junk food binge with friends, I returned home with a dreadful stomachache. My aunt, being ever the eco-holistic evangelist, introduced me to her world of natural remedies, grounding exercises, and meditation. It was not just about curing that singular pain, but understanding the intricate balance our bodies share with the environment.

Here's what I've learned, both from Aunt Marge and my years of diving deep into eco-holistic health:

- **Listen to Your Body:** Just as the environment sends signals (like climate change) when it's out of balance, our bodies do the same. Recognizing these signals early can save a lot of pain later.

- **Natural Remedies:** Before reaching for over--the-counter medicines, see if there's a natural remedy. Ginger tea for sore throats, lavender oil for better sleep, or turmeric for inflammation. The earth has a lot to offer if we just know where to look.

- **Mind-Body Connection:** Yoga, meditation, grounding exercises. These aren't just buzzwords. They genuinely help in aligning our physical health with our mental well-being.

- **Educate Yourself:** The more you know, the better choices you make. Not just for your health, but for the environment as well.

If this topic has kindled a spark in you (and I hope it has!), there's a book I'd recommend: "The Nature Cure: Why Nature is the Best Medicine for Both Body and Mind" by Andreas Michalsen. It's a brilliant dive into the world of eco-holistic health. And, for an even deeper dive, consider online courses or joining eco-holistic tribes. There's a treasure trove of knowledge out there waiting to be explored!

Keep the curiosity burning and remember: our health and the planet's health are intertwined in more ways than one. Cheers to a holistic journey!

So, diving into some practical advice? Sure thing:

- **1.Start Small**: Don't dive headfirst. Introduce one change at a time into your lifestyle. Maybe begin with switching to organic food or using eco-friendly cleaning products.
- **2. Stay Informed, But Not Overwhelmed**: It's easy to drown in information today. Subscribe to a couple of reliable eco-health newsletters or channels but give yourself a break too.
- **3. Remember Your 'Why'**: On challenging days, remind yourself why you started this journey. Was it for your health? The planet? Both?

Mood swings and feelings of melancholy,or anxiety aren't uncommon as we age. The pressures of health, the pain of lost peers, or even the simple solitude can weigh on one's spirit. But, nestled within the very soil we walk upon are mood-lifting remedies. St. John's Wort, a yellow-flowered plant, has been tapped for centuries for its potential to treat mild to moderate depression. The delicate Lavender, with its calming aroma, can lull a troubled mind to peace. Just as the sun breaks through the darkest clouds, these natural remedies shine a light on our moodiest days.

Rekindling Vitality

With age might come a slight decrease in zest and energy. Ginseng, an ancient root, is well known for its energy-boosting properties. Similarly, Maca, a root vegetable hailing from the Andes, has long been consumed for increased stamina and energy. Nature, it seems, has a way of replenishing our dwindling reserves, injecting vigor where it's most needed.

The Touch of Time

The touch of time on our skin is perhaps the most visible. Wrinkles, age spots, and the loss of elasticity become our new companions. But in the heart of nature, we find oils and herbs that nourish and rejuvenate. Aloe Vera, known as the 'plant of immortality' by the ancient Egyptians, hydrates and heals. Coconut oil, rich in fatty acids, offers moisturization. Nature embraces us, telling us that beauty is ageless, timeless.

Nature's Symphony: An Ongoing Dance with Time

If we pause to look a bit deeper, beneath the canopy of leaves and the sprawling meadows, we find that the entire natural world is intertwined in an intricate dance of symbiosis, growth, and rejuvenation. As we step into our golden years, it's not just about finding remedies, but about tuning into this dance, syncing our rhythms to the heartbeats of the earth, and realizing that we're part of a larger, awe-inspiring ballet of existence.

- **Restful Slumbers and Dreams:** Sleep patterns often shift as we age. Some may find it harder to fall asleep, while others might wake up frequently throughout the night. Again, nature extends her gentle hands to cradle us into restful slumbers. Chamomile, a dainty flower resembling a daisy, has been brewed into teas for millennia, known to calm the mind and ease one into sleep. Valerian root, too, has been a trusted ally for those seeking deeper, more restful nights.

- **Eyes, The Windows to Our Soul:** Over time, our eyes, those deep pools of emotions and experiences, may start to betray signs of wear. Vision might get clouded, or the sparkle may diminish. But there's the magic of bilberries, closely related to blueberries, believed to improve night vision, and maintain healthy eyes. Similarly, carrots, with their rich content of beta-carotene, aren't just an old wives' tale; they genuinely support eye health.

- **Heart's Whispers:** The heart, that tireless pump and the emblem of our emotional world, too, faces the brunt of age. But Hawthorn berries, with their rich red hue, have been utilized in traditional medicine to support cardiac health. Omega-3 fatty acids, abundantly found in flaxseeds and fish like salmon, also play a pivotal role in maintaining heart health. It's as though nature herself is reaching out, holding our heart, and whispering, "I've got you."

· **Gut Instincts:** Digestive issues often crop up with age. As metabolism slows, and as the body's internal balance shifts, we might find ourselves grappling with indigestion or a sluggish system. But lo and behold, natures got an answer for that too! Ginger, with its spicy kick, aids digestion and combats nausea. Peppermint, either in tea or as an oil, can soothe an upset stomach.

· **Final Reflections:** Every stage of life, be it the exuberance of youth or the reflection of the golden years, is a chapter in the story that nature has been narrating since time immemorial. Each remedy, each solution she offers is a verse in this grand epic.

Embracing Mother Nature's remedies isn't just about seeking cures. It's about a deeper communion with the earth. It's about understanding that, even as the sands of time slip through our fingers, we are held, supported, and cherished by the planet we call home. The golden years aren't a time of decline but of deepening – a time to sink our roots into the rich soil of life and draw nourishment, just as the ancient trees do.

In nature, we find a mirror, reflecting not just our vulnerabilities but our inherent strength and resilience. As we sail into the sunset of our lives, with Mother Nature as our compass, the voyage promises to be one of discovery, serenity, and profound connection.

Aging is a natural process that everyone undergoes, bringing about various physiological, psychological, and biochemical changes. While modern medicine has solutions for many age-related ailments, traditional and natural remedies have been trusted for centuries and can effectively manage and prevent some of these issues. Here are some Ayurvedic natural remedies for common ailments that people face as they age:

1. Arthritis and Joint Pain:

- **Turmeric and Ginger:** These have anti-inflammatory properties and can be consumed as teas or supplements.
- **Green tea:** Rich in antioxidants, it can reduce inflammation and slow cartilage destruction.

2. Digestive Problems:

- **Peppermint:** Can help soothe digestive discomfort and reduce bloating.
- **Fennel seeds:** aid digestion and alleviate gas and bloating.

3. Memory and Cognitive Decline:

- **Ginkgo Biloba:** It's believed to boost memory and cognitive function.
- **Rosemary:** This herb is associated with improved memory. It can be consumed as a tea or used in cooking.

4. Insomnia and Sleep Disorders:
· **Chamomile:** Known for its calming properties, chamomile tea can promote sleep.
· Valerian root: Acts as a natural sedative and can help induce sleep.

5. Cardiovascular Health:
· **Garlic:** Helps in reducing cholesterol and blood pressure.
· **Flax seeds:** Rich in Omega-3 fatty acids, they help reduce cholesterol and promote heart health.

6. Vision Decline:
· **Bilberries:** Rich in antioxidants, they can improve night vision and prevent macular degeneration.
· **Carrots:** They contain beta-carotene, which is beneficial for eyesight.

7. Osteoporosis:
· **Blackstrap Molasses:** High in calcium and magnesium, it helps in supporting bone health.
· **Sesame Seeds:** Rich in calcium, they can be sprinkled on foods to boost bone health.

8. Urinary Tract Issues:
· **Cranberry juice:** It prevents bacteria from adhering to the urinary tract walls, reducing the risk of infections.
· **Pumpkin seeds:** They can help maintain a healthy prostate and reduce symptoms of an enlarged prostate.

9. Skin and Hair Issues:

· **Aloe Vera:** Provides hydration and has anti-inflammatory properties for the skin.

· **Coconut oil:** is a natural moisturizer that promotes healthy hair and skin.

10. Depression and Mood Swings:

· **St. John's Wort:** Often used as a natural remedy for depression.

· **Omega-3 Fatty Acids:** Found in fish oils and walnuts, they can help regulate mood and reduce depression.

While these natural remedies can be beneficial, it's important to note that they should be taken after consulting with a healthcare provider. Natural remedies can interact with medications or conditions, making it imperative to ensure their safe consumption.

The journey of aging, while natural and inevitable, comes with challenges encompassing physical, cognitive, and emotional dimensions. Many societies, particularly those with strong ties to traditional knowledge systems, have developed many natural remedies to counteract or alleviate these challenges. Here are some natural remedies that can help mitigate aging-related issues:

1. Cognitive Decline:

· **Brahmi (Bacopa monnieri):** Used traditionally in Ayurvedic medicine, it has shown the potential to enhance cognitive functions and memory.

· **Ashwagandha:** Known for its adaptogen properties, it helps combat stress, which can significantly affect cognitive decline.

2. Skin Aging:

· **Olive oil:** Packed with antioxidants, it can be applied topically to prevent wrinkles and skin dryness.
· **Cucumber slices:** Applied over the eyes, they can reduce puffiness and dark circles.

3. Hair Thinning and Graying:

· **Amla (Indian gooseberry):** A powerhouse of antioxidants, it can be used as oil or in powdered form to nourish the hair and prevent premature graying.
· **Fenugreek seeds:** Can be used as a hair mask to prevent hair loss and promote growth.

4. Reduced Energy and Vitality:

· **Ginseng:** Known for its rejuvenating properties, it can enhance stamina and energy.
· **Maca root:** Often taken in powdered form, it helps increase energy and endurance.

5. Bone Health:

· **Nettle tea:** Rich in calcium and magnesium, it supports bone health.

· **Dandelion greens:** Packed with calcium, they can be incorporated into diets to support skeletal health.

6. Hormonal Imbalance:

· **Black Cohosh:** Often used to manage menopausal symptoms.
· **Chaste Tree Berry (Vitex):** Helps in balancing female hormones.

7. Digestive Issues:

· **Triphala:** An Ayurvedic blend of three fruits, it aids in digestion and detoxification.
· **Probiotic-rich foods:** Foods like yogurt, kimchi, and sauerkraut help maintain gut flora, which is essential for digestive health.

8. Cardiac Health:

· **Hawthorn berries:** Traditionally used to support heart health.
· **Arjuna bark:** An Ayurvedic remedy is known for its cardio-protective properties.

9. Muscle and Joint Pain:

· **Eucalyptus oil:** When massaged, it is a natural pain reliever for joint and muscle pain.
· **Willow bark:** contains salicin, a natural precursor to modern-day aspirin.

10. Mood and Emotional Well-being:

· **Lavender:** Its essential oil or even the dried flowers can be used for their calming and mood-elevating properties.

· **Passionflower:** Often consumed as a tea, it can help reduce anxiety and promote calmness.

Incorporating these natural remedies can offer a holistic approach to aging, targeting the causes rather than just the symptoms. However, it's crucial to consult with healthcare professionals before starting any regimen, as natural doesn't always mean safe for everyone, especially considering potential interactions with other medications or health conditions.

The vast repository of nature and traditional knowledge systems offers promising solutions to the multifaceted challenges posed by aging. Harnessing them judiciously can pave the way for graceful and healthy aging.

In Conclusion, while aging is inevitable, the associated ailments can be managed, alleviated, or even prevented with modern medicine and trusted natural remedies. Embracing a holistic approach toward health can help ensure a better quality of life as one ages.

It's heartening to realize we're not alone as we navigate our golden years. Nature, with her vast canvas of remedies, stands by our side, a testament to the cycle of life. Each herb and plant offer more than just a remedy; they connect to the earth, reminding us of the rhythm of life.

We find an echo of our existence in every whispered wind through the willow trees and every ray of sunshine that nurtures the turmeric. The wear and tear of our golden years isn't merely an end but a beautiful transition, one that Mother Nature herself aids, soothes, and celebrates.

In Conclusion

As we navigate our golden years, it's heartening to realize that we're not alone. Nature, with her vast canvas of remedies, stands by our side, a testament to the cycle of life. Each herb, each plant, offers more than just a remedy; they provide a connection to the earth, reminding us of the rhythm of life.

In every whispered wind through the willow trees, in every ray of sunshine that nurtures the turmeric, we find an echo of our existence. The wear and tear of our golden years isn't merely an end but a beautiful transition, one that Mother Nature herself aids, soothes, and celebrates.

Chapter 2

 As our world evolves, how can the wisdom of eco-holistic health guide our footsteps to a heartwarming, ageless vitality?

Mother Nature's Gifts: Soothing the Wear and Tear of Our Golden Years

Amarin's life was full of vitality, and as she grew older, she noticed wrinkles forming on her face and her hands becoming unsteady. Nevertheless, her spirit remained resilient. At the age of 80, she moved to a quaint cottage that overlooked sprawling green fields and majestic mountains.

As age-related ailments began to take their toll, Amarin found comfort not in medication or treatments but in the natural beauty that surrounded her. She believed the land was vital to soothing her aching joints and fatigued spirit.

Each morning, Amarin would step barefoot into her garden, relishing the sensation of dew-kissed grass beneath her feet. The moist soil between her toes felt like a soothing massage from Mother Nature, rejuvenating her soul and evoking memories of her childhood playing in the fields.

She would brew tea from chamomile and mint that she grew herself. The freshly plucked herbs seemed to melt away her worries and pains, warming her from the inside out.

In the afternoons, she would sit by the brook that flowed behind her house. The gentle gurgling of the water had a way of speaking to her, whispering secrets of resilience and the importance of facing every obstacle with unwavering determination.

But Amarin's favorite remedy was the evening ritual she had adopted. She would collect fallen leaves, dried petals, and twigs, grinding them together to make a powder. Mixing the powder with honey collected from the beehive in her yard, she'd create a mask for her face and hands. The concoction would soothe her wrinkled skin, making it feel revitalized.

One day, a young girl from the village named Lakhmi visited Amarin. She had heard of the old lady who refused to succumb to the effects of aging. Lakhmi found Amarin in her garden, laughing as she danced under the sun, her silver hair flowing freely.

"Please teach me," Lakhmi said, "**how to age like you**."

Amarin took Lakhmi's hand, leading her to a small patch where she grew lavender. "Life will give you wrinkles, my dear," she said, plucking a sprig and placing it in Lakhmi's palm. "But nature will give you remedies. Not to erase the years but to celebrate them. Each line is a tale, and each ache is a memory. Embrace them, soothe them, but never resent them."

As the sun set, casting a warm golden glow over the fields, Amarin and Lakhmi sat together, basking in the natural beauty around them. It wasn't just a lesson on aging; it was a lesson on living. To let nature's gifts, heal and nurture us as we navigate the tapestry of life woven with threads of experience.

Greetings readers! Today, I'd like to discuss the phase of life that we all aspire to reach - the golden years. As we age, our hair turns silver, and our pace slows down, but these years often reflect the stories we've written throughout our lives. However, the wear and tear of age and experience accompany these stories. The good news is that Mother Nature has always been ready to accompany us on this journey.

The art of life involves embracing the challenges and joys that every stage of life brings. As we enter our golden years, nature comes closer, offering remedies that can help us along the way.

Most of us have experienced a nagging backache or joint pain after a particularly strenuous day. That's where willow and turmeric come in - nature's very own aspirin, with the power to alleviate those aches. And as we grow older, who has yet to walk into a room occasionally and forget why? While I might joke about having a "senior moment," herbs like ginkgo biloba and rosemary stand by to bolster our memory.

Emotionally, our golden years can be a roller coaster. The changing dynamics of life can affect our moods. Here again, nature plays a therapist. St. John's Wort and the soothing scent of lavender can help balance our moods and soothe our spirits.

But what about the spirit itself, the very essence of who we are? As we age, we begin to appreciate the more profound, more tactile experiences of life. Have you ever walked barefoot on grass, feeling its cool embrace? Or touched the soft petals of a flower, marveling at its delicacy? These simple treasures become profound joys. Practices like shinrin-yoku or forest bathing, immerse us in the silent embrace of trees, grounding us in the present moment.

The golden years are not just about looking back at the life we've led. They are an invitation. It is an invitation to experience life deeply, to connect with our surroundings, and to embrace the wisdom that nature has to offer.

So, as we navigate the intricacies of aging, let's remember that we're not alone. With every step, sigh, and chuckle, nature is right there, offering her remedies, comfort, and boundless wisdom.

In our golden years, let's dance with nature, rejuvenate with her remedies, and cherish the wisdom of the ages. Because age is not just a number - it's a celebration. And nature? She's the life of the party. Thank you.

The Sacred Ties: Weaving Nature into our Daily Art

As we sail forth into the uncharted water of tomorrow, the depth of eco-holistic health emerges not just as an alternative but as a fundamental necessity. This wisdom, gentle yet profound, compels us to intertwine the threads of nature into our daily art, ensuring a richer, more vibrant pattern of existence.

- **The Essence of Balance:** Balance, in its purest form, is at the heart of eco-holistic health. In an age where multitasking is revered, where 24/7 connectivity is the norm, we often find our scales tilting dangerously towards burnout. Yet, the wisdom of nature urges equilibrium. From the ebb and flow of tides to the changing seasons, nature operates in cycles of activity and rest. By emulating this natural rhythm, by carving out moments of stillness amidst our busy lives, we recharge and revitalize. This might mean digital detox weekends, afternoon siestas, or simply moments of quiet contemplation.

- **Nature's Classroom: Lifelong Learning** : One of the pillars of enduring vitality is continuous learning. And what better teacher than nature herself? Engaging in activities like bird watching, botanical studies, or stargazing doesn't just expand our knowledge but connects us deeper to the world around. Nature's classroom is vast, ever evolving, and infinitely enriching. Every leaf, every cloud, every gust of wind holds lessons of resilience, adaptability, and harmony.

- **The Alchemy of Community:** Humans, by nature, are social beings. The eco-holistic approach celebrates community, recognizing that collective well-being fuels individual vitality.

Community gardens, eco-villages, and group nature retreats are not just recreational activities. They foster a sense of belonging, a shared purpose, and a mutual reverence for the earth. In these gatherings, stories are woven, wisdom is exchanged, and the age-adage of 'it takes a village' is lived and relished.

• **Therapeutic Arts and Crafts:** Returning to our roots often means rekindling forgotten arts. Pottery, using the very clay of the earth, or weaving, employing nature's fibers, are therapeutic outlets. They allow hands and hearts to create in tandem with nature's bounty. Such crafts are not mere hobbies; they're a communion, a rhythmic dance of creation that keeps the spirit youthful and agile.

• **Sacred Rituals:** Incorporating nature-based rituals into our daily routine amplifies our connection to the universe. This could be as simple as lighting natural incense, practicing sunrise yoga, or moonlit meditations. These rituals anchor us, providing a consistent touchpoint with the sacredness of existence.

• **Final Thoughts:** In this intricate ballet of existence, as our world whirls and waltzes into the future, the wisdom of eco-holistic health is our steadfast partner. It ensures that our steps are grounded, our movements graceful, and our vitality undiminished. By weaving nature into our narrative, we don't just survive; we thrive, heartwarming ageless in our dance with the cosmos.

Deepening Our Roots: The Eco-Holistic Odyssey Continues

As we journey through the annals of our existence, the eco-holistic paradigm serves as a reminder that our true essence is intrinsically linked with the universe. Every breath we take, every step we make, is a harmonious symphony with the cosmos. And as this odyssey continues, the richness of our connection only deepens, inviting us to explore realms previously uncharted.

- **Guardians of Nature's Legacy:** In a world racing ahead, often at the cost of environmental sanctity, adopting an eco-holistic lifestyle transforms us into stewards of nature. The guardianship isn't about dominion but about reverence. By creating and participating in conservation initiatives, whether it's a local cleanup drive or supporting global reforestation projects, we play an active role in healing our planet. This act not only rejuvenates our environment but replenishes our own spirit.

- **Digital Era, Timeless Connection:** The advent of the digital era presents a paradox. On one hand, it risks distancing us from the palpable touch of nature; on the other, it holds the power to unite eco-conscious communities worldwide. Virtual platforms can become hubs of knowledge-sharing, where the wisdom of one corner of the globe enlightens another. Online workshops on traditional herbal remedies, virtual tours of world forests, or collaborative eco-art projects are ways in which technology bridges the physical-digital divide, keeping the eco-holistic flame alive.

· **Cycles of Renewal:** Nature thrives in cycles. The shedding of autumn leaves paves the way for spring's renewal. Similarly, our lives, especially as we age, are marked by endings and beginnings. Eco-holistic wisdom teaches us to embrace these transitions, seeing them not as losses but as opportunities for rebirth. Rituals celebrating milestones, like an eco-friendly retirement party or a nature-bound ceremony for life achievements, integrate the beauty of life's cycles into our personal narratives.

· **Mindful Consumption:** In a consumer-driven society, the choices we make significantly impact our health and our environment. An eco-holistic approach advocates for conscious consumption. This could translate to supporting sustainable brands, reducing waste, or even the simple act of savoring a meal, acknowledging the journey of each ingredient from earth to plate. Every act of consumption then becomes an act of gratitude.

· **Symbiotic Growth:** Lastly, as we cultivate our personal gardens of well-being, we realize that growth is most vibrant in symbiosis. Mutual growth, whether it's fostering a community garden, mentoring the younger generation in eco-practices, or collaborating on green initiatives, ensures that the eco-holistic legacy thrives and evolves.

· In Reflection : The path of eco-holistic health is not a destination but a continuous voyage. As the contours of our world shift and reshape, this timeless wisdom adapts, always relevant, always nurturing. By deepening our roots, we not only anchor ourselves in ageless vitality but also become the beacon of light for generations to come, ensuring that the heartwarming dance with nature never fades.

Absolutely! Incorporating eco-holistic health into one's daily life can benefit both the individual and the environment. Here are some actionable tips that readers can integrate into their routines:

1. **Herbal Remedies and Recipes:**
    · Tea Blends: Create homemade teas using herbs.
    · like chamomile, mint, or ginger. These are natural stress relievers and digestion aids.
    · Natural Sleep Aids: Consider using herbs like valerian root or lavender to promote a restful sleep.
    · Herbal Salves: Use ingredients like calendula, comfrey, or plantain to make salves that can help minor skin irritations.

2. **Eco-friendly Products:**
    · Reusable Containers: Instead of single-use plastics, use stainless steel or glass containers for storing food and beverages.

· Natural Cleaning: Use natural cleaning agents like vinegar, baking soda, or lemon instead of chemical-based cleaners.

· Sustainable Fashion: Buy clothing from ethical and sustainable sources. Consider materials like organic cotton, hemp, or bamboo.

3. **Nature-based Activities:**

· Nature Walks: Start or join a local walking group that explores nearby nature trails or parks.

· Community Gardening: Join or start a community garden. This allows for the cultivation of organic vegetables and fosters community spirit.

· Eco-crafting: Use natural or recycled materials to create crafts. For instance, you can make decorations from fallen leaves or create artwork using driftwood.

4. **Eco-Holistic Practices:**

· Meditation in Nature: Find a quiet spot outdoors to meditate, helping to connect you to the environment and find inner peace.

· Eco-yoga: Practice yoga outside or in eco-friendly studios. Use yoga mats made from sustainable materials.

· Nature Journaling: Keep a journal of your observations and feelings as you spend time in nature. This can deepen your connection to the environment.

5. **Join or Support Local Eco-Groups:**
   · Conservation Groups: Join local organizations focused on conservation efforts, tree planting, or wildlife protection.
   · Eco-Workshops: Attend or host workshops on sustainable practices, like composting, permaculture, or rainwater harvesting.
   · Farmers' Markets: Support local organic farmers by buying produce from farmers' markets. This reduces the carbon footprint linked with long-distance transportation of goods.

6. **Eco-friendly Home Practices:**
   1. Composting: Start a compost pile or bin in your backyard or community to recycle organic waste.
   2. Rainwater Harvesting: Set up systems to collect rainwater, which can be used for watering plants or even as greater in the household.
   3. Green Energy: Consider installing solar panels or using energy providers that incorporate renewable sources.

Here are the key takeaways from the written.
Piece on the eco-holistic approach to an evolving world:

1. **Intrinsic Connection:** The essence of eco-holistic health is understanding our deep interconnectedness with nature and the universe.

2. **Nature as Stewardship:** Adopting an eco-holistic approach transforms individuals into active stewards and protectors of the environment.

3. **Balancing Digital and Natural:** While the digital age offers numerous conveniences, it's essential to maintain a tangible connection with nature. Technology can be used to foster global eco-communities and share knowledge.

4. **Life's Natural Cycles:** Embracing life's transitions and recognizing them as opportunities for growth and renewal is a hallmark of eco-holistic wisdom.

5. **Conscious Choices:** Mindful consumption, whether in terms of food or consumer goods, can profoundly impact personal health and the environment.

6. **Community and Symbiotic Growth:** The eco-holistic approach emphasizes community-building and collaborative efforts for mutual growth.

7. **Legacy and Mentorship:** Passing down eco-holistic values and practices ensures the sustainability of this philosophy for future generations.

8. **Nature as Teacher and Healer:** Engaging in activities that connect us to nature fosters continuous learning and provides therapeutic benefits.

9. **Rituals and Traditions:** Incorporating nature-based rituals into our lives helps anchor

us and serves as touchpoints of gratitude and reflection.

10. **Embracing Wholeness:** True health isn't just physical well-being but a harmonious balance of mental, emotional, and environmental health.

The eco-holistic approach offers a roadmap for individuals to navigate the challenges of a rapidly evolving world, ensuring they maintain ageless vitality and a deep, nourishing connection to nature.

Chapter 3:

In the quiet whisper of the trees and the gentle ripple of the brooks, how can we find secrets to rejuvenating our mature spirits?

Whispers of Rejuvenation: Nature's Melody to the Mature Soul

Marjorie had always found solace in the rhythmic hum of the city. For over six decades, that symphony of car horns, distant chatter, and the occasional roar of a subway train had been the soundtrack of her life. But lately, the once comforting noises began to grate on her spirit, leaving her yearning for a change she couldn't quite articulate.

On a whim, Marjorie booked a small cabin in the mountains of Himalayan Kingdom, devoid of Wi-Fi or the incessant ping of notifications. Her children were alarmed. "You, Mom? In the middle of nowhere?" But she had made up her mind.

As Marjorie approached the cabin, the familiar clatter of urban life faded, replaced by the gentle rustling of leaves, the chirping of crickets, and the subtle murmur of a distant stream. Her heart, tense from years of hustle, began to ease its grip.

She awoke to a symphony unlike any she had ever heard the first morning as sunlight peaked through the gaps in the drapes. Birds serenaded the new day, their melodies pure and untainted by the ambient noises she was used to. The whispering wind carried secrets from distant lands, and the trees swayed gracefully, beckoning her to join in their dance.

She stepped outside, her bare feet greeted by the dewy grass. The scent of pine and wildflowers flooded her senses. With every deep breath, the mountain air seemed to rejuvenate her mature soul, peeling away layers of fatigue and worry.

Days blended seamlessly. Marjorie lost track of time, her usual routine replaced by unhurried walks, hours spent reading by the babbling brook, and peaceful nights under the stars. The vastness of nature, with its intricate designs and patterns, whispered ancient wisdom to her. She realized how small and fleeting human concerns were in the grand tapestry of the universe.

One evening, as the sun set behind the mountains, casting a golden hue on the landscape, Marjorie sat by the brook, her toes playing with the cool water. A soft melody emanated from the forest's depths, a tune that spoke directly to her heart. It sang of rebirth, renewal, and the timeless cycle of life. The mountains, trees, and rivers had seen countless sunrises and sunsets, yet with each new day, they found a way to be reborn.

Marjorie returned to the city with a transformed spirit. The cacophony of urban life no longer overwhelms her. Instead, she carried the whispers of the mountains within her, a constant reminder of nature's rejuvenating power. The melodies she had discovered resonated deeply, providing solace and wisdom to her mature soul.

Moreover, so, in the heart of the bustling city, Marjorie found a way to dance to nature's tune, her spirit forever rejuvenated by the whispers of the wild.

Below the Canopy of the Silk Route Forest: A Rejuvenation for the Mature Soul

Hello dear reader! Have you ever felt like life is moving too fast? Sometimes, we must remember to stop and enjoy the journey instead of focusing on the destination. Today, I want to take you through a beautiful forest. This forest is not just a bunch of trees and plants; it's a place to reconnect with nature and find peace and calmness.

The Silk Route Forest is a magical place where time seems to stand still. The air is filled with a sense of ancient and new wonder. Walking through this forest is like entering a unique world where every tree has a story to tell. The trees are likewise old sages, gently whispering secrets about the universe.

Just imagine the leaves of these ancient trees. They have seen so much history and change over the years. Each leaf has a story about endurance, growth, and resilience. Walking through the forest, you'll see the sunlight filtering through the trees, creating beautiful patterns on the forest floor. It's a reminder of the different shades of life and how we can learn from them.

Walking through the forest, you'll hear the gentle sound of a nearby brook. The water flows over the pebbles, singing a song of renewal. It's a beautiful melody that inspires introspection. There's a sense of stillness in the forest that reflects the peace within our own souls.

It's not just about what you see in this forest. It's also about what you hear, smell, and feel. The sound of the rustling leaves and the gentle murmur of the brook create a soothing lullaby that speaks directly to the heart. The scent of the earth after a fresh rain or the feeling of moss-covered stones beneath your feet are experiences that awaken the senses.

In this forest, you'll find a purity and authenticity you might have forgotten. It's an invitation to reconnect with nature and let go of the stresses of everyday life. The Silk Route Forest is a sanctuary where you can find rejuvenation and peace. Nature is always there to remind us that we can find wisdom and renewal in the world around us.

So, I encourage all of you to find your own special place in nature, wherever that may be. Take the time to enjoy the journey and discover the boundless wisdom and renewal that nature can offer. Thank you for sharing this journey with me!

Nature's Timeless Embrace: A Continuum of Soulful Rediscovery

I can relate to your childhood memories of bees buzzing around a banyan tree. I can imagine the sight of those vibrant and busy bees hovering over the tree's hanging roots and enjoying the sweet nectar of its flowers. It's a beautiful image that reminds us of the intricate and interconnected relationship between nature's creatures and the plants they rely on for survival. It's also a reminder of the simple pleasures of childhood and the wonder and joy of exploring the world around us.

Beyond the known pathways and the familiar landmarks, where the forest deepens and the realm becomes almost otherworldly, one steps into a theater of nature's purest performances. It's a place where every element, from the wind's gentle caress to the Earth's steadfast embrace, is in a delicate choreography crafted for the solace of mature hearts and spirits.

Imagine, for a moment, the experience of standing at the edge of an age-old glade. The trees here stand tall and wise, their trunks bearing the marks of countless seasons, each scar a testament to resilience, each ring a chapter of stories untold. They've witnessed epochs, yet time seems to dissolve in their presence. One feel wrapped in an ageless embrace, as if these guardians of nature hold within their core the essence of life and timelessness.

Gentle beams of sunlight pierce the verdant canopy between the trees, creating pools of golden warmth on the forest floor. Each beam is like nature's soft touch, it's way of caressing and assuring the mature spirit that in this place, amidst this serenity, one can shed the weight of worldly timelines and simply be.

The symphony continues with the occasional flutter of a butterfly, its iridescent wings capturing fragments of light, reminding us of the fleeting yet beautiful moments that life gifts us. Or the distant echo of a woodpecker rhythmically conversing with a tree, a reminder that even in solitude, there's a vibrant dialogue waiting to be experienced.

But perhaps the most entrancing of all is the serenade of the brooks. These delicate waterways, with their clear, crystalline flows, are like the arteries of the forest, pulsating with life. They carry within them tales from the mountain peaks to the vast oceans. As one sits by a brook, feet dipped in its cool embrace, there's an immediate sense of connection—a flow of energy, a melding of ancient wisdom. It whispers secrets of embracing change, letting go, and the perennial promise of rejuvenation.

Every petal, every gust of wind, every shadow, and every silhouette in this ethereal grove invite introspection. It's a call to rekindle the spirit, breathe deeper, listen more intently, and rediscover oneself in the embrace of nature's ageless art.

As one emerges from this haven, there's a palpable lightness—a sense of having communed with the eternal, of having sipped from the elixir of life itself. The mature spirit, bathed in nature's alchemy, feels rejuvenated and deeply connected, ready to dance once more to the ever-evolving rhythm of existence.

The Mystical Dance of Nature: An Immersion into the Soul's Abyss

Hey there, fellow seeker of the dance of nature!

"The Mystical Dance of Nature: An Immersion into the Soul's Abyss" immediately caught my attention, reminding me of a winter evening a few years ago when I went backpacking alone in the forests of the Northeast of India, Manas. As the Sun began to set and a gentle stream flowed beside my camp, I had an unforgettable encounter with the dance of nature.

Suddenly, a faint glow caught my attention as I settled for dinner. Fireflies. But not just a couple—thousands dancing in a mesmerizing ballet around me. It felt as if they were inviting my soul to join them in the dark abyss of the universe, waltzing alongside their silent melody. That night, I realized how deeply intertwined the rhythm of nature is with our personal journeys. Our souls are intrinsically linked to this dance; every time we immerse ourselves in it, we find another fragment of our true selves.

The best way to dive into this immersion is to actively engage with nature. You don't have to go solo to a remote forest (although I highly recommend it!). You can start with simple activities, like walking in a local park without headphones. Feel the breeze, listen to the birds, and be in the moment. You can also create a ritual, perhaps a daily meditation routine, where you visualize yourself as part of this vast universe, feeling every pulse and rhythm. Over time, you'll perceive the world around you in a new light.

I hope this resonates with you. I wish you an incredible journey ahead as you unravel the mystical dance of nature!

In a secluded pocket of the world, where mankind's footprints are scarce and nature unfolds in its rawest form, lies a realm untouched by time's relentless march. It's a sanctum so deep and profound that one cannot merely observe but must surrender, letting the soul plunge into its depths.

A palpable hush envelops you as you enter this ancient, primal forest. It isn't just the absence of noise but a silence that speaks volumes—the kind of silence that is heavy with wisdom, waiting for the receptive ear. Every rustle of the leaf, every distant call of a hidden creature, resonates like an echo from an age when Earth was young and untamed.

The trees here are not mere plants; they are the very pillars of the universe, their roots delving deep into the mysteries of the Earth, their branches reaching out, intertwining with the cosmos. Their bark bears the etchings of countless tales, of storms, weathered and seasons embraced. Beneath their protective shade, one feels a profound connection, as if listening to the world's heartbeat.

But it's the waters that genuinely beckon. Hidden brooks, their courses charted eons ago, flow with an almost surreal clarity. To approach one is to stand at the edge of introspection. Gazing into its depths, one doesn't just see the shimmering reflections but gazes into the soul's very abyss. The water, ever-flowing yet ever-still, mirrors life's paradoxes. Its gentle murmurs whisper the ancient secrets of balance, of embracing life's dualities — the ebb and flow, the joy and sorrow, the birth and decay.

Amidst this, there's a scent in the air, an aroma that's not just of the damp Earth or the blooming flowers but something more ethereal. It's the fragrance of time itself, a reminder of the transient nature of existence and the eternal continuum of the universe. Breathing it in is akin to absorbing the essence of life, a potion that revitalizes the spirit and awakens dormant memories of past lifetimes.

And as night descends, the canopy above comes alive. Like the memories of ancient sages, myriad stars twinkle with stories from the dawn of creation. The vastness of this cosmic art, juxtaposed against the intimate embrace of the forest, creates a duality where one feels infinitesimal yet integral, fleeting yet eternal.

In this profound communion with nature, the mature spirit finds more than just rejuvenation. It discovers a deeper layer of existence, a dimension where every atom, every whisper, and every shadow are imbued with meaning. The journey into this forest is not merely a walk but a pilgrimage, an odyssey into the core of being, where one emerges refreshed but transformed with a soul that has touched the infinite.

Hey there, kindred spirit! Your question resonated profoundly and reminded me of a personal story I've never publicly shared.

The question resonated deeply with me and reminded me of a personal story that I've never really shared publicly.

Here are the key takeaways from the narrative on Nature's Timeless Embrace:

1. **Nature's Theater:** The depth of the forest is likened to a stage where every element performs in harmony, providing solace for matured hearts.

2. **Trees as Timekeepers:** The ancient trees in the forest symbolize resilience and timelessness, with each mark and ring holding stories from epochs gone by.

3. **Sunlit Assurance:** The beams of sunlight piercing through the canopy are nature's way of comforting and reminding one of the warmth and constancy in change.

4. **Beauty in Fleeting Moments:** Elements like the fluttering butterfly emphasize the transient yet profound beauty in life's fleeting moments.

5. **Brooks as Life Carriers:** The brooks, acting as the forest's arteries, encapsulate tales from various landscapes, urging introspection and embracing change.

6. **Connection and Flow:** Being in nature, especially by the water, fosters a deep sense of connection, facilitating energy transfer and wisdom sharing.

7.   **Invitation for Introspection:** The forest and its elements invite individuals to delve deep within, promoting self-reflection and a rejuvenation of the spirit.

8.   **Emergent Lightness:** After experiencing the forest's magic, one emerges feeling lighter, having communed with the eternal and being ready to embrace life's dance anew.

Chapter 4:

How can embracing the beauty of nature enhance our well-being and paint our twilight years with colors of joy?

In the art of life, a hidden atelier exists where nature serves as the palette. For those who dare to enter this sacred space, the twilight years become a canvas bursting with vibrant hues and limitless possibilities.

Picture a meadow at dawn, where dew kiss's petals that shimmer in the morning light. Each drop reflects a universe of color, and the flowers themselves are not just flora but the strokes of a masterful artist. They convey tales of resilience, rebirth, and radiant beauty. Walking through this sea of blossoms, the air seems to pulse with energy, infusing the spirit with a renewed sense of wonder.

Further on lie ancient forests, where sentinel trees stand tall like guardians of legends and traditions. Whispers between leaves carry secrets of joyous celebrations, storms weathered, and seasons embraced with grace. The dappled sunlight filtering through the canopy dances on one's skin, each ray painting away the aches and worries that come with time's passage.

Beside a tranquil pond, reflections tell tales of clarity and introspection. Gazing upon this mirrored surface means journeying inward and discovering reservoirs of joy and happiness that time cannot tarnish. The gentle ripples created by a passing breeze, or a solitary fish urge us to embrace the flow and find harmony in the dance of existence.

Nature's palette is not solely visual. The symphony of birdsong at daybreak, the lilting lullaby of crickets at twilight, the gentle caress of a mountain breeze, or the intoxicating aroma of blooming jasmine under a silvered moon - these are nature's hues, painting our souls with profound emotions and reminding us of the boundless beauty that life holds.

In embracing nature, we don't just witness beauty; we immerse ourselves in it. This communion enhances our well-being, both physically and ethereally. As the sun sets on our journey, casting the world in a golden-orange glow, our twilight years become a masterpiece. Every moment is a vibrant splash of joy; every memory is a testament to a beautifully lived and cherished life.

Thus, as age graces us with wisdom and experience, nature offers its gift: a palette to paint our days with colors so vivid and profound that our twilight becomes a radiant dawn, a promise of joy everlasting.

Nature's Symphony: The Resplendent Overture to Life's Final Act

Ameli sat on a rock and looked out at the unadulterated, primordial, untouched valley below. The river reflected the colors of the sunset, creating a beautiful art of oranges, purples, and gold. The world was coming alive, preparing for the most beautiful symphony she would ever hear.

Behind her, she heard the soft cooing of doves and the distant sound of a waterfall, creating a delicate beginning to the evening's performance. As the sun set, the cicadas joined in, adding to the melody. In a language that man has forgotten, legends, and traditions but that nature has remembered, the wind rustled the leaves and whispered secrets.

Ameli loved music and had attended many concerts and operas, but they were nothing compared to this wild and untamed orchestra. Here, there was no conductor or rehearsed notes, only the unrestrained harmony of life.

Her doctor told her she had little time left a few weeks ago. Instead of giving in to sadness, she decided to embrace life and set out to find nature's purest melody. And so, she embarked on a pilgrimage, searching for a place untouched by time, far away from the noise of city life.

As the night fell, the stars twinkled in rhythm with the fireflies that danced around her. The nocturnal creatures began their part, deepening the richness of the symphony. Each sound was distinct but blended seamlessly with the next, creating a perfect balance of highs and lows.

Ameli felt the world around her, not just with her ears but her soul. She felt a profound connection to everything around her, as if the melodies of nature resonated with the rhythm of her heartbeat, connecting her to the world in ways she had never imagined.

As dawn approached, the valley slowly awoke from its nocturnal trance. The symphony began to soften, giving way to the gentle hum of the morning. The sky transformed from a deep blue to hues of pink and gold, signaling the concert's end.

Ameli's heart was whole. She had found what she had come looking for, not just in the sounds of the night but within herself. She realized that the symphony of nature was not just an overture to life's final act but a testament to the timeless beauty of existence itself.

And with that, Ameli let go, becoming one with the world around her, her soul joining the eternal dance of nature's symphony.

Beyond the known horizons, where the mundane gives way to the magnificent, lies an uncharted realm, one where nature's embrace envelops the soul with an intensity that is both gentle and profound. For those poised at the threshold of life's final act, this embrace transforms the impending twilight into a crescendo of vibrant experiences, each more vivid than the last.

If you will, picture an old-growth forest, its atmosphere thick with tales of past epochs. The moss-covered floor, soft and plush, invites the weary traveler to tread gently, each step cushioned like a whispered secret between ancient friends. Towering trees, their boughs laden with myriad green shades, rise like nature's cathedrals, casting kaleidoscopic patterns as sunlight filters through their leaves.

Deep within this sanctuary, a hidden glade awaits, a clearing where beams of sunlight converge, painting the ground with golden filigree. The air here vibrates with a tangible energy, every breath infused with the earthy scent of ferns and the subtle perfume of wildflowers, creating a art of aromas that tantalize and rejuvenate the senses.

Amidst this setting, the symphony of nature unfolds. A brook babbles with joyous abandon, its waters leaping over stones, glistening like a thousand diamonds in the midday sun. Birds, draped in plumage that would put the finest tapestries to shame, serenade with melodies that tug at the heartstrings, their songs echoing the timeless dance of life and love.

As the day wanes, the heavens, too, join this grand performance. The horizon, painted in amber, rose, and indigo shades, becomes a canvas of dreams as stars emerge like countless fireflies, each twinkling with stories from the vast cosmos. Under this celestial canopy, one feels a profound connection, a realization that even as the pages of one's story near their end, the narrative is eternally woven into the fabric of the universe.

Nature's embrace, so full of sensory wonders, serves as a balm for the body and a salve for the soul. The rustling leaves share tales of hope, the cascading waterfalls echo with laughter, and the vast meadows, awash with colors, remind us that beauty and joy are not confined to youth but are the constant companions of those who seek them with an open heart.

Thus, as the curtain prepares to descend on life's grand play, nature steps in as the maestro, orchestrating a glorious finale so imbued with wonder that one's twilight years are transformed. They become not an ending but an overture to a song that resonates beyond time, a hymn of joy, gratitude, and boundless beauty.

Whispers from the Cosmos: Nature's Luminous Dance with Eternity

On a distant planet named Luminara, where the trees shone with bioluminescent splendor and the oceans glowed under the diamond-dusted sky, the inhabitants had a unique way of communicating with the cosmos.

The Lumineers, as they were known, were a race of ethereal beings who communicated through a series of harmonic vibrations. These harmonies were not merely sounds but radiant pulses of light, painting the air with the colors of their emotions, dreams, and memories. The Lumineers had perfected a celestial symphony, and every evening, they would gather at the Grand Amphitheater, the highest point on Luminara, to share the whispers of the cosmos.

As the two moons of Luminara converged on the horizon, Lyria, a young Lumineer, approached the Grand Amphitheater. She had been practicing a new harmony, one she believed held the secrets of eternity. As she began her luminous dance, her vibrational melodies merged with the ethereal glow of Luminara's landscape. With every movement and note, she felt as if she were caressing the very fabric of time.

As the Lumineers witnessed Lyria's performance, they saw a dance and a story. The first moon's glow depicted the stars' birth and the vibrancy of life emerging and evolving. The light of the second moon showcased the eventual fading of stars, the beautiful yet sad twilight of existence.

Suddenly, a pulse of brilliant white light emanated from the core of Luminara, reaching out to the farthest galaxies. The Lumineers watched in awe as an intricate pattern of lights responded from the vast expanse of the universe, shimmering in acknowledgment of their shared cosmic connection.

These were the echoes of ancient civilizations, long gone, their stories now interwoven with those of the Lumineers. And as the light show culminated in a grand crescendo, every Lumineer felt an overwhelming sense of unity—with one another, Lyria, and the infinite cosmos.

In that moment, Lyria understood that beginnings or endings did not bind the dance of life. It was an eternal waltz where the past, present, and future melded in a luminous embrace. Nature's radiant performance celebrated this endless cycle, a dance with eternity itself.

As Luminara's two moons rose again the next day, a new harmony was added to the Lumineers' repertoire. It was a testament to the night when they had all danced with the cosmos and felt the eternal embrace of nature's luminous dance with eternity.

And so, on a distant glowing planet, the whispers of the cosmos continued, reminding every Lumineer of the beauty, wonder, and timeless dance of existence.

In the vast, uncharted expanse of existence, where time weaves its intricate art and the cosmos spins tales of the ancient and the infinite, there lies a realm of profound resonance. It's a dimension where nature's cadences meld seamlessly with the soul's deepest yearnings, casting the twilight years not as a quiet fading but as a luminous crescendo, echoing with the profound mysteries of the universe.

Welcome, dear readers, to a journey through the boundless realms of content, imagination, and emotional connections. We will explore the magic that allows stories and experiences to transcend their mere words and touch the human heart.

Just a moment ago, you were transported to a world where time seemed to stand still. Nature and the cosmos intertwine, creating a tapestry of wonder and profundity. The scenes were painted vividly, making you almost feel the wind, hear the rustle, and touch the waters of that ethereal grove. But what was this journey? Was it just a string of words or content in its purest form?

Content is more than just pieces of information. It is a bridge between realms, a connection that can transport us from the ordinary to the extraordinary. When crafted with authenticity and emotion, content can make us feel alive, remind us of our humanity, and make us yearn for more.

In this modern age, we are constantly bombarded with information. Amidst this deluge, we often crave content that truly resonates, speaks to our soul, and takes us on a journey.

The story I shared at the beginning is not just a portrayal of nature or the cosmos. It is a reflection on life, the fleeting nature of our existence, and the awe-inspiring tapestry of experiences that we, as humans, are privileged to be part of. As we age, such content can serve as a reminder that every moment is precious and that the dance with eternity is ongoing.

Think about the stories that have touched you. Perhaps a novel that made you cry, a movie that made you laugh, or a song that made you feel alive. That is the power of content. It does not just inform; it transforms. It does not just narrate; it resonates.

So, whether you are a creator, a reader, or just an observer, let us strive for content that transcends the superficial. Let us yearn for stories that take us on journeys, remind us of our humanity, and challenge us to think and feel deeply.

In the embrace of such profound content, we find a sanctuary – a place where the soul dances, the heart beats in joy, and the mind soars to infinite possibilities.

Examples:

1.**Nature Walks and Mental Health:** Consider the Japanese practice of "Shinrin-Yoku" or "forest bathing." Regular practitioners often report improved mood and reduced stress levels. In Japan, there are specific trails designated for this practice where individuals immerse themselves in nature, taking in the surroundings through all their senses.

2.**Urban Green Spaces:** Cities like Singapore have integrated green spaces into urban planning. These areas, such as the Gardens by the Bay, offer city-dwellers a respite from the hustle and bustle, providing opportunities for relaxation and recreation.

3. **Community Gardens and Social Well-being:** In many communities, gardening has been shown to foster

not just individual well-being but also community cohesion. Planting and tending to a garden can be therapeutic, and the resulting produce can be a source of pride.

Experiments:

1. Reduced Stress Levels: A study from the University of East Anglia synthesized data from over 140 studies involving more than 290 million people. It found that exposure to green spaces reduces the risk of type II diabetes, heart disease, and high blood pressure. Additionally, living close to nature and spending time outside has significant and wide-ranging health benefits.

2. Improved Concentration: A study published in the journal "Environmental Science & Technology" found that children with ADHD who played regularly in green settings had milder symptoms than children who played in built outdoor and indoor settings. This suggests that nature can be beneficial in improving concentration.

3. Boosted Immune Function: Research has indicated that individuals who spend time in nature, especially forests, exhibit increased production of natural killer cells, which are vital for our immune system and fighting disease.

<u>**Key Takeaways:**</u>

1. **Life as Art:** The twilight years can be viewed as a canvas, offering limitless opportunities to paint vibrant experiences and memories inspired by the beauty of nature.

2. **Nature's Resilience:** Nature, in its myriad forms from blossoms to ancient forests, tells tales of resilience, rebirth, and radiant beauty, reminding us of the enduring spirit present in all of life.

3. **Deep Introspection:** Tranquil spots in nature offer opportunities for introspection, allowing one to connect with the depths of their soul and discover untarnished joys and happiness.

4. **Sensory Symphony:** Nature's palette goes beyond visuals—it encompasses sounds, scents, and touch, which profoundly impact the soul and elicit deep emotions.

5. **Well-being through Communion:** Immersion in nature enhances holistic well-being, rejuvenating the body and the spirit.

6. **Timeless Nature's Embrace:** Nature's embrace offers a perspective transcending time. With it, one's later years become a testament to a beautifully lived life rather than an ending.

7. **Nature's Universal Symphony:** Nature is the world's most natural and harmonious orchestra, where

every creature and element plays its unrestrained part in the harmony of life.

8. Eternal Connection: Nature serves as a conduit connecting individuals to the vastness and mysteries of the cosmos, suggesting that even as life nears its end, one remains eternally interwoven with the universe.

9. Celestial Communication: On Luminaria, the Lumineers' use of harmonic vibrations to communicate with the universe embodies the idea that nature and the cosmos can commune in profound, indescribable ways.

10. The Dance of Eternity: The journey of life is not bound by beginnings or endings. It's an ongoing dance with the cosmos and a luminous embrace with eternity, full of wonder and boundless beauty.

11. Nature as a Cosmic Reflection: Nature mirrors the vastness and enigma of the cosmos, offering glimpses into the more profound mysteries of existence, suggesting that life's twilight is not an ending but a radiant overture to the dance of eternity.

12. Soul's Sanctuary in Nature: By attuning to nature's rhythms and the vast cosmos, the soul finds solace, rejuvenation, and an eternal dance of joy and wonder.

The overarching message from the narrative is that nature, in all its grandeur, offers a profound perspective on existence. Whether in the blossoming of flowers, the ancient tales of towering trees, or the harmonious melodies of distant planets, nature reminds us of life's boundless beauty and infinite possibilities. Embracing it, especially in the twilight years, transforms life's final act into a luminous dance with eternity.

Chapter 5:

What ancient, earth-rooted practices can help the elderly feel more connected, grounded, and cherished in today's fast-paced world?

Whispers from the Earth

In the heart of New York City, amid its towering skyscrapers and the ceaseless din of traffic, there was a small community garden, a patch of green squeezed between buildings. Locals named it 'The Oasis'. Its very existence was a protest to the relentlessness of modernity.

Elena, a spry 87-year-old with silver hair, was the guardian of this verdant alcove. She had witnessed the world change in unimaginable ways. Technology had made life easier and the world smaller, but a sense of disconnection came with that ease. People, especially the elderly, felt left behind, trying to anchor themselves amidst the digital chaos.

One morning, Elena gathered the elderly residents of the neighborhood. They sat in a around a freshly dug pit in the garden. She began to share stories of ancient, earth-rooted practices like stories of silkworm to weaving, long forgotten in the cacophony of the digital age.

"Centuries ago," she began, "our ancestors felt a bond with the Earth. They understood nature's rhythms, cycles, and silent whispers. Today, we'll embrace one such practice."

She spoke of 'tree-talking'. (The natural world and fostering a deep sense of connection). In many indigenous cultures, talking to trees was a way of grounding oneself. The elderly were encouraged to find a tree in the garden, touch its bark, and share their stories, fears, and joys.

As the days turned into weeks, this ritual became a refuge. Elena explained, carried the wisdom of the ages. By sharing with them, the elderly felt seen, heard, and cherished.

Elena introduced more practices. 'Earth breathing' was another. They would sit on the ground, close their eyes, and imagine the breath of the Earth merging with theirs. This rootedness gave them strength.

Every Friday was a 'song of memories,' where the elderly sang songs from their youth. These melodies, spanning decades, connected them to their past, making them realize they were a link in the unbroken chain of humanity.

One day, a young tech entrepreneur named Leo, who had recently moved to the city, stumbled upon The Oasis. He approached Elena because the rituals intrigued him. Witnessing the serenity and sense of community, he realized that while the world championed innovation, it sometimes overlooked the simple, profound wisdom of the past.

Leo and Elena collaborated, intertwining the ancient with the modern. Using technology, they broadcast 'The Oasis' rituals worldwide, making them accessible to every elderly individual feeling lost in the digital shuffle.

The world took notice. Soon, pockets of green and serene spaces started appearing in cities everywhere. Elders gathered, touched trees, sang old songs, and breathed with the Earth.

The ancient rituals did not repel technology; instead, they merged, reminding the world of the importance of roots in an ever-advancing age.

And in the heart of New York City, an old woman with silver hair smiled. The world was fast paced, but in the whispers of the Earth, everyone found their rhythm.

Hello! reader, Tonight, I'd like to transport you to a space where time flows differently, where the old and the new dance in harmony, and where the elderly find solace in practices as ancient as the stars.

We live in a world that often feels like a perpetual sprint. The blinking notifications, the rush of traffic, the rapid, incessant beat of modern life. In this symphony of progress and noise, it's easy to feel disconnected. Especially for our elders, those who have witnessed the turn of eras and the changing tapestries of life, the cacophony can sometimes be overwhelming.

But, my friends, there is a different kind of music that beckons—a song of the Earth, of tradition, of age-old practices that cradle the soul and reconnect us to our roots.

Take pottery, for instance. There's a magic in the way hands meet clay, in how the spinning wheel becomes a temporal portal, connecting the potter to generations past. For the elderly, this isn't just crafting; it's a communion—a tangible link to a world where patience and artistry matter more than instant gratification.

Or consider the verdant embrace of a forest. In Japan, they've known for years about the therapeutic wonder of 'Shinrin-yoku' or forest bathing. For the elderly, these ancient woods aren't just a backdrop; they're a living testament to endurance and transformation. A walk among the trees is not just about movement but about being moved, about being one with a world much larger than oneself.

The beauty of these practices is that they aren't solitary pursuits. In the heart of the community, around crackling fires, our elders, the venerable storytellers, bring history alive, recounting tales of valor, love, and mystery. Their voices, infused with years of experience, become the very heartbeat of our lineage, ensuring that stories are not lost in the sand of time.

And then, in the fragrant embrace of herbs and blossoms, the elderly practice a form of healing that transcends the physical. As they blend potions and brews, they honor a relationship with nature, serving as a bridge between the ancient wisdom of the Earth and the needs of the present.

In essence, the fast-paced world we've constructed is full of spaces for our elders. Earth-rooted practices beckon, offering them a haven. It's up to us to listen, to engage, and to celebrate these threads that connect us to our past, grounding us firmly in the rich tapestry of life.

As we leave today, let's carry with us a commitment to honor, cherish, and engage with these traditions, ensuring that our elders and we remain eternally connected to the soul of the world.

Echoes of Earth's Wisdom: A Journey to Ancestral Grounding

"Echoes of Earth's Wisdom: A Journey to Ancestral Grounding" deeply resonated with me. I still vividly recall the spring I backpacked in the Himalayan Mountains not too long ago. While exploring the misty peaks, I discovered an old village where the community still honored the traditions passed down through generations. One night, an elderly woman shared with me the stories of their ancestors, which instilled in them a profound connection with the Earth, the stars, the Silk Route, the Yetis, and everything in between. She spoke of a grounding energy, a wisdom from the Earth that their community tapped into for guidance and resilience. This experience significantly impacted me, causing me to re-evaluate the fast-paced lifestyle of city living and seek more grounded experiences.

Now, drawing from that experience and my expertise, here are some practical tips for you:

· **1. Nature Walks:** Take regular walks in nature, whether it's a park, forest, or beach. Use this time to connect with your surroundings. Listen to the rustle of leaves, feel the ground beneath your feet, and immerse yourself in the moment.

· **2. Ancestral Stories:** Explore your own family history. Talk to your grandparents or elders. Understand their struggles, joys, and the wisdom they carry. You'll be amazed at how much you'll learn about yourself.

· **3. Mindfulness and Meditation:** It might sound cliche, but meditation has its roots in ancient traditions. Find a practice that resonates with you, perhaps grounding meditations that connect you to the energy of the Earth.

· **4. Community:** Engage in community activities that promote ancestral connections. This could be attending workshops, joining spiritual groups, or organizing gatherings to share stories.

There is a fantastic book by Robin Wall Kimmerer called "Braiding Sweet grass" if you're really into deep diving. It beautifully intertwines indigenous wisdom, science, and the teachings of plants.

I encourage you to embark on this fascinating journey and rediscover the echoes of Earth's wisdom. The quest for ancestral grounding isn't just about connecting to the past but also understanding our place in the present and the legacy we want to leave for the future. Happy exploring!

Welcome, fellow readers, to a journey that will take us back to the very core of our being. In today's world, where technology pervades every aspect of our lives, it's easy to lose touch with the timeless wisdom that has guided us for centuries. But there is a realm beyond the noise, a place where the spirits of our elders still roam, waiting for those who seek their guidance.

Picture a serene lake nestled in the embrace of ancient mountains. Here, our elders come to wash away the noise of the world and cleanse their souls in the waters that hold the memories of ages past. It's a place of profound connection, where the grand narrative of existence weaves itself into the present moment.

Or imagine the vast deserts, where the echoes of caravans still linger in the wind. Our elders, draped in robes, journey forth alone, seeking visions and clarity. Amidst the unyielding expanse of the sky, they find revelations that bridge the generations, fortifying the spirit and reminding us of our place in the grand scheme of things.

And then there are the gardens, with their winding paths and intricate patterns. Our elders walk these labyrinths, each step a deliberate reminder of the journey of life. Memories resurface, dreams awaken, and gratitude fills the heart, reminding us that life, with all its twists and turns, is a dance of purpose and beauty.

Finally, as the night sky unfolds above us, our elders lie back and drink in the spectacle of the cosmos. In that stillness, they understand that they are threads in the vast tapestry of existence, just like the eternal stars above. It's a reminder that the boundless spirit within them is mirrored in the infinite wonder of the universe.

In a world where technology often drowns out the heartbeat of our planet, these ancient practices are a lifeline. They anchor the soul and offer a bridge to the timeless, the profound, the sacred. Let us cherish and preserve them so that future generations can find their way back to the heartbeat of the Earth and honor the wisdom of our ancestors.

In Earth's Profound Embrace: An Odyssey Through Time's Sacred Heartbeat

In Earth's Profound Embrace: An Odyssey Through Time's Sacred Heartbeat" truly moved me! It brought back a remarkable memory of mine related to this fascinating subject. A few years back, I had the opportunity to explore the Thar Desert, which left me spellbound with its vast expanse. One night, while gazing at the starry sky, a local guide, Ramu, shared stories of ancient nomads who believed that the desert's vastness reflected the timeline of Earth itself. He gifted me an hourglass that looked like it was from the Ashoka kingdom, with each sand grain representing thousands of years passed. Watching the sand trickle down, I felt connected to everything around me. Each grain of sand beneath my feet and each gust of wind carried whispers from history, reminding me of the Earth's sacred rhythm and our fleeting existence within it.

Navigating Earth's temporal embrace is a philosophical and physical journey. Here are a few paths you might tread:

· **1.** **Ancient Sites:** Exploring ancient civilizations, like the Mayans, Egyptians, or the Indus Valley, offers insights into humankind's early perceptions of time. In their unique ways, these cultures recognized and celebrated Earth's rhythm.

· **2. Nature Retreats:** Spend time in places untouched by modern civilization - deep forests, deserts, or mountain ranges. Being in these spaces can shift your perspective, making you feel immensely insignificant and deeply connected to the planet.

· **3. Astrology & Astronomy:** Understanding the cosmic dance can provide context to Earth's place in the vast universe. Dive into the intricacies of star movements and planetary alignments. Their ageless journey offers a glimpse into the vastness of cosmic time.

For further exploration, I'd highly recommend the book "Cosmos" by Carl Sagan. It beautifully interweaves the universe's journey with Earth's evolution and humanity's quest for understanding.

Hello, dear readers. Today, I invite you on a journey with me, far away from the hustle and bustle of our modern world and into the depths of time itself.

Our world is filled with technology and constant notifications, making it easy to get lost in the maze of digital life. However, there is another reality, timeless and abundant, where the stories of the past call out to us, especially as we enter the golden years of our lives.

Imagine standing during an ancient forest, surrounded by moss-covered stones laid out in mysterious patterns, echoing the hum of the universe. For the elderly, these stones whisper stories, weaving their own life's tale with the eternal ballads of the cosmos. This is a place where time doesn't just pass; it dances, inviting the soul to join in.

Deep within the Earth's core, caves with walls adorned with memories of epochs gone by beckon us to explore. Imagine our elders' holding torches, casting light upon scenes of primordial life. In the dance of shadows and firelight, the boundary between then and now blurs. They are not just observers but become a part of a story that has been unfolding since the dawn of time.

Picture high mountain peaks, where silence is a tangible entity. Here, hidden monasteries echo with chants that resonate with the pulse of existence itself. Our elders, immersed in this melody, find a rhythm that ties them to the boundless universe, awakening a realization of life's cyclical nature and eternal flow.

Finally, in the vast desert, where the world seems but a whisper, the elderly connects with the cosmos. Drawing patterns in the sand under a canopy of stars, they find reflections of their own life's journey. The limitless horizon mirrors the vast spirit, affirming that even as they near life's twilight, they are an essential note in the grand symphony of existence.

Friends, while the allure of modern life is undeniable, let's not forget the ancient echoes that call out to us, reminding us of our eternal connection to the universe. As we, or our loved ones, approach the later chapters of life, let's cherish these sacred practices. They are not just rituals; they are bridges connecting us to the very heart of existence, offering not an ending but a profound beginning.

In the embrace of these ancient rhythms, our elders, and all of us, discover a truth: that we are, and always have been, woven into the vast, beautiful tapestry of the cosmos.

Thank you for joining me on this journey today. Cherish the dance of time, embrace the rhythm, and find your place amidst the stars.

To deepen your connection to these ancient rhythms, here are some take ways:

- **1. Star Gazing:** Spend time under the open sky, observing the constellations. Understand that these patterns have been witnessed by countless generations before you.

- **2. Ancient Rhythms:** Engage in traditional dances or music. These often carry stories and philosophies that have been passed down over millennia.

- **3. Sacred Sites:** Visit places revered by ancient cultures. Whether it's

Stonehenge, Machu Picchu, or the Pyramids, these sites connect us to ancient understandings of our place in the cosmos.

• **4. Commune with Nature:** Spend uninterrupted time in nature, be it forests, oceans, or mountains. Listen to its whispers and recognize its timeless wisdom.

Chapter 6:

As we look back at a lifetime of memories, how might the wonders of eco-holistic health help us craft a soul-nourishing journey ahead?

Whispers of Yesteryear's: The Art of Eco-Holistic Futures

Elena sat on her porch, surrounded by the tranquility of a small village nestled between rolling mountains by Dal lake. She was the village's oldest resident at 98 years old, and her memories spread before her like a art of stories, each thread representing a moment, a feeling, and a lesson. As Mina, a young and enthusiastic student of eco-holistic health, visited her, Elena saw in her the passion and curiosity of youth and the potential to carry on her legacy.

Mina had come with a request, eager to learn from Elena's experience. "Tell me, Elena, how did the practices of eco-holistic health shape your journey?" she asked, drawn in by the wisdom and vitality that emanated from the older woman.

Elena smiled, her eyes glistening with the memories of a lifetime. "It wasn't just about the herbs, meditations, or yoga, my dear Mina. It was about understanding the delicate balance between our souls, the environment, and the cosmos."

Elena's voice was filled with warmth and nostalgia as she began to recount her life. She spoke of her childhood when she woke up to the chirping of birds instead of the jarring sound of an alarm clock. She remembered the wildflowers she would pick, each with a unique medicinal property, a secret her grandmother had shared. "We didn't just consume the plants," Elena reminisced, "We respected them and understood that taking also meant giving back."

Elena sought refuge in nature during her most challenging times as a young woman, grounding herself through barefoot walks on dew-laden grass. "The Earth has a rhythm," she explained to Mina, "and when you connect with it, your heartbeats synchronize with the universe."

With age, Elena embraced a holistic approach to facing health challenges. Ancient breathing techniques, herbal concoctions, and moonlit meditations became her allies. The village often wondered how Elena, even in her 90s, had the vitality of someone half her age.

Mina listened with rapt attention, deeply engaged in the stories of a life well-lived. She realized that eco-holistic health was not just about physical practices but encompassed a way of life and an understanding of the interconnectedness of the natural world.

Finally, Mina asked, "What's the secret, Elena? How can I create a soul-nourishing journey ahead?"

Elena leaned forward, her eyes sparkling with mischief. "Dear Mina, it's not about adding years to your life but life to your years. Listen to nature, for it speaks. Breathe in synchrony with the world. Love deeply, not just people, but every leaf, every pebble. And always remember, holistic isn't just a practice; it's a way of life."

As the sun began to set, casting a warm glow over the mountains, Mina left Elena's porch, feeling a profound connection to Elena and the timeless wisdom of the universe. She was inspired to live a life that was not just healthy but also meaningful and fulfilling, a life that was in harmony with nature and the cosmos.

Greetings, dear readers. Today, I invite you to join me on a journey of self-discovery, where we can take a moment to reflect on the beauty of our lives. Imagine a breathtaking sunset casting a warm glow upon our memories. As we stand at this introspective horizon, we're faced with a thought-provoking question: how can we make the rest of our life's journey as fulfilling as the stories that lie behind us?

Close your eyes and visualize a peaceful forest where every leaf, every twig, sings a song of wisdom. It's in this embrace of nature that we discover the wonders of eco-holistic health, a philosophy that merges the rhythms of the world outside with the pulse of the world within us.

Imagine a serene pond nestled amidst this green sanctuary, reflecting the present moment with gentle ripples. This embodies meditation and mindfulness, allowing us to cherish every nuance and sensation of the now.

As we continue our forest stroll, we're greeted with the sweet scent of herbs, each with its own tale and healing properties. Lavender, chamomile, and other plants are not just remedies for physical well-being but also a spiritual connection, promoting holistic harmony.

Soon, we hear the distant sound of voices and come across a heartwarming sight - a group of people, young and old, gathered around a fire, sharing stories, laughter, and music. This is the essence of eco-holistic health, where our personal journey is also a shared adventure. In togetherness and community, we find a collective strength.

Let's embrace this eco-holistic approach to living, integrating nature's wisdom, the beauty of the present moment, the healing properties of plants, and the power of community. Together, we create a roadmap for a life filled with harmony, purpose, and deep joy.

As we continue our journey through life, may the principles of eco-holistic health light our path, ensuring that every step we take resonates with love, gratitude, and a profound appreciation for the interconnected dance of existence.

Thank you for accompanying me on this exploration today. May your path be illuminated with understanding, and may your heart always find its rhythm in the sacred dance of life.

Harmonies of Healing: A Serenade to Eco-Holistic Resonance

The topic "Harmonies of Healing: A Serenade to Eco-Holistic Resonance" immediately caught my attention and reminded me of a personal experience I would like to share. A few springs ago, I decided to take a solo retreat in the serene highlands of Kashmir valley, where I hoped to find peace, tranquility, and a deeper connection with nature. The beauty of the landscape was breathtaking, and I found myself immersed in the sights, sounds, and scents of the natural world.

One evening, as the sun slowly descended over the horizon, painting the sky in vivid hues of orange and pink, I found myself on the edge of a still Dal Lake. The only sounds around me were the distant cry of an eagle and the gentle ripple of water, creating a sense of peace and serenity that I had never experienced before.

Suddenly, I felt a strong urge to hum a tune that matched nature's rhythm. As I closed my eyes and let my voice blend with the sounds of the environment, I felt a deep connection with the Earth and the living creatures around me. It was as if the Earth, in turn, was echoing my tune and healing me with every note while I, in turn, serenaded it with gratitude.

The experience was transformative, and I felt a renewed sense of purpose and connection with the natural world. It was a genuine moment of eco-holistic resonance, where nature and I healed each other harmoniously.

Now, to foster such harmonies in our lives, it's essential to tap into the healing rhythms of nature. Here are some pointers:

- **1. Sound Baths:** Incorporate natural soundscapes into your routine. Be it the murmur of a forest, the crash of ocean waves, or the soft drizzle of rain, these sounds have been proven to aid relaxation and healing.

· **2. Nature Immersion:** Regularly spend time in nature. Take off your shoes, feel the grass, hug a tree, or lie under the open sky. These simple acts can ground you and forge a deeper connection with the Earth.

· **3. Meditative Music**: Explore music that integrates natural sounds. Instruments like the didgeridoo, Tibetan singing bowls, or even the Native Tibetan flute can evoke feelings of being one with nature.

I'd highly recommend the book "The Sound of Healing" by Michael Tyrell for a deeper dive. It beautifully captures the essence of healing through frequencies and harmonies. Platforms like Insight Timer offer meditative tracks that blend music with nature sounds, facilitating a journey of eco-holistic resonance.

My friend, nature sings a continuous song of healing and harmony. Sometimes, all we need to do is pause, listen, and join in the serenade. It's a dance of mutual healing as ancient as the Earth itself.

Hello! Have you ever taken a moment to appreciate the beauty of the horizon and the connection it holds between the earth and the sky? It's a reminder of our past and a glimpse of what's to come. I invite you to join me on a journey guided by the universe's melodies and the wisdom of eco-holistic health.

Imagine walking into a vast meadow filled with living colors and beautiful yellows and whites. Each petal is a testament to nature's rejuvenating touch. Breathing in the air full of blooming flowers' perfume will lift a weight off your shoulders, leaving you with an indescribable sense of peace.

Listen to the cheerful giggles of the brook as it winds its way through the landscape. It's nature's elixir, offering the healing embrace of hydrotherapy. Playing with its shimmering surface will wash away your fatigue, stress, and sorrow, rekindling the flames of vitality within.

In a secluded nook, surrounded by nature's verdant shawl, you'll find a sacred space. Here, the age-old practices of yoga and tai chi come to life. As you stretch, move, and breathe, your soul aligns with the planet's heartbeat.

As the day turns to night, a circle of kindred spirits gathers. Here, tales of yore and dreams of what lies ahead intermingle. Oral traditions, a fundamental pillar of eco-holistic health, ensure our shared experiences are etched into the annals of time.

My dear friends, as we journey through life, let us remember that our future is not just a continuation of the past. Instead, with eco-holistic health as our guiding star and nature as our trusted companion, we can create a beautiful masterpiece with the universe. Infuse your journey with the vibrancy of nature's wisdom, ensuring that every step you take resonates with harmony, gratitude, and boundless wonder.

Thank you for sharing this moment with me. Remember to dance to the rhythm of nature, letting its songs guide your heart and its wisdom illuminate your path.

The Elysian Ode: A Timeless Stopover with Nature's Timekeeper

Topic "The Elysian Ode: A Timeless Stopover with Nature's Timekeeper" brings back a vivid memory of a beautiful experience in my life. Some years ago, while exploring the ruins of an old **Sun Temple**, I stumbled upon an ancient sundial. It was nestled amid the ruins, and I was fascinated by its unique design. Intrigued, I decided to learn more about it and unravel its secrets.

The elderly janitor of the temple noticed my interest and beckoned me to come closer. He started sharing stories and legends surrounding the sundial, which he called **"Nature's Timekeeper."** He explained how it was believed to synchronize with the sun and the Earth's heartbeat. As the sun's rays cast shadows, marking time, people would come to meditate, finding themselves transported to a realm where time seemed to dance to nature's lyrical ode.

The janitor's tales piqued my curiosity, and I decided to spend an afternoon exploring the sundial's mysteries. As I sat by the sundial, I felt a sense of calm and peace envelop me as though I was cocooned in an Elysian bubble. I was transported to another world where every moment felt fleeting and eternal. The world buzzed with energy, yet I felt connected to the universe's rhythm.

In summary, encountering "The Elysian Ode: A Timeless Stopover with Nature's Timekeeper" was a life-changing experience for me. It gave me a glimpse into a realm where time and nature are intertwined, and every moment is fleeting and eternal.

For those looking to embark on their own timeless journey with nature, here are some routes to explore:

· **1. Shadow and Light:** Play with the duality of nature. Sunrise and sunset, often called the golden hours, are moments when nature seems to pause, inviting us to join in its reflective dance.

· **2. Natural Timekeepers:** Embrace nature's chronometers. This could be the rhythmic crash of waves, the shifting shadows of a sundial, or even the silent bloom of flowers that open and close with the sun.

· **3. Mindful Moments:** Dedicate moments in your day to be fully present. Whether watching a leaf drift to the ground or observing the intricate dance of fireflies, immerse yourself completely.

For those eager to delve deeper, "Circles in Time: Reflections in Nature's Rhythms" by David T. George is must-read. It masterfully captures the interplay of time and nature, offering readers a lens to view the world in its timeless splendor. Platforms like Masterclass have mindfulness and nature meditation courses that could provide the tools and insights you're seeking. Lastly, joining or creating a community around 'nature mindfulness' can be incredibly rewarding, offering shared experiences and collective wisdom.

Hello, reader. Think we are gathered here, surrounded by the wonders of technology and modern advancements, let's take a moment to appreciate the beauty of our planet.

Nature teaches us a valuable lesson - it operates on a calm and steady rhythm, untouched by the hustle and bustle of our daily lives. The changing seasons, blooming flowers, and rising sun all happen on nature's own timeless schedule. This rhythm is the core principle of eco-holistic health, encouraging us to adopt it.

Just imagine an ancient forest that has stood the test of time. The majestic sequoia trees have seen empires rise and fall and the evolution of species. They tell the story of Earth's history in the rings of their trunks. Deeper into the forest, you might find a spring - the source of life itself. Drinking from it is like being one with history and the essence of our planet.

In a twilight-lit glade, elders perform ancient rituals that blend breath and movement. This dance blurs the boundary between self and cosmos, embodying grace, and wisdom. Eco-holistic health is about realizing that we are both finite and infinite beings.

As the darkness envelops the forest, the elders tell stories of profound connection, touching the divine and understanding the intricate tapestry of life. These stories connect the past and future, weaving visions of a world where man and nature are one.

Our lives might feel finite, but through eco-holistic health, every heartbeat and breath become a bridge to the infinite. By aligning ourselves with nature's timeless rhythm, we don't just exist, but we truly live. Our days have become an ever-expanding dance with the cosmos.

Ultimately, understanding our place in the universe requires us to listen, feel, and dance to the symphony of Earth and stars. With eco-holistic health as our guide, our journey becomes not just meaningful but transcendent.

Thank you for joining me on this exploration. May your paths always resonate with the songs of the Earth and the echoes of the stars.

Eco-Holistic Health: An Inclusive Approach to Total Well-being

Health is no longer just about the absence of illness but rather a balance of mental, physical, and environmental well-being in today's fast-paced world. Eco-holistic health is a sustainable and comprehensive approach that connects nature with individual wellness. This approach promises a more profound and long-lasting health benefit.

Body-Mind-Nature Connection

Eco-holistic health is based on the idea that our bodies are intrinsically connected to the environment. This means that we draw nourishment not only from the food we eat but also from the air we breathe, the water we drink, and the landscapes we surround ourselves with. It's a holistic approach emphasizing the importance of maintaining a healthy relationship with nature for our overall well-being.

Benefits of Eco-Holistic Health:

· **Enhanced Mental Health:** Natural settings have a unique, rejuvenating effect on the human psyche. Studies have repeatedly shown that even a short time in nature can decrease feelings of anxiety, depression, and anger. Forest bathing, a Japanese practice known as shinrin-yoku, is a testament to this. Immersing oneself amidst trees can significantly elevate mood and mental clarity.

· **Stress Reduction:** The modern world is rife with stressors. Eco-holistic health practices emphasize activities like grounding (walking barefoot on natural surfaces), which can help reduce cortisol levels, the body's primary stress hormone. The gentle sounds of nature—birdsong, flowing water, rustling leaves—act as natural relaxants, calming the overactive mind.

· **Improved Sleep Patterns:** Exposure to natural sunlight during the day and reduced exposure to blue light (from screens) in the evening can help reset the body's circadian rhythm. Camping for even a weekend, away from artificial light, can significantly improve sleep quality and duration.

· **Holistic Nourishment**: Eco-holistic health advocates for consuming organic, locally sourced, and seasonal foods. This reduces the carbon footprint and ensures that the body receives nutrients at their peak freshness and potency.

· **Emotional Resilience:** Engaging with nature often involves adapting to unpredictable patterns. This adaptability can foster emotional resilience, enabling individuals to better navigate life's ups and downs.

· **Enhanced Immunity:** Regular interaction with natural environments exposes the body to various microorganisms, bolstering the immune system. Moreover, specific practices, like herbal remedies, tap into nature's vast pharmacy to boost health and ward off illnesses.

Embracing an eco-holistic approach to health ensures a life of harmony within ourselves and the world around us. It's an invitation to slow down, tune in, and rediscover the ancient wisdom of unity and balance. For those on the precipice of their wellness journey, this path offers profound healing rooted in the rhythms and cycles of Mother Earth.

By integrating these benefits and the science behind them, the writing becomes informative and persuasive, encouraging readers to delve deeper into eco-holistic health practices.

Here are the key takeaways from "The Elysian Ode: A Timeless Sojourn with Nature's Timekeeper":

1. Nature as Time's Testament: The ancient sequoias serve as monumental timekeepers, their rings capturing epochs of Earth's history, connecting our transient lives to eternal rhythms.

2. Nature's Elixir: The pristine springs in the heart of the forest symbolize rejuvenation and connection to Earth's primordial essence, emphasizing the therapeutic and spiritual connection we can forge with the natural world.

3. Harmonizing Breath with Being: The practice of ancient rituals like qi gong and pranayama in the forest glade represents the union of body and spirit, reminding us of the age-old methods that ground us and connect us to the universe.

4. Eternal Stories Underneath the Stars: The gathering of the elderly under the constellated night sky signifies the interweaving of past wisdom and future visions, highlighting the cyclical and interconnected nature of life.

5. Spiraled Odyssey of Existence: Our life journey is depicted not as a straight line but as a spiraled exploration, where we repeatedly delve deeper into cosmic mysteries, merging our fleeting existence with the universe's eternal dance.

6. Depth Over Duration: The essence of the narrative is the idea that through eco-holistic health and alignment with nature, our lives, while finite in days, can attain an immeasurable depth

and resonance, transcending temporal constraints.

In essence, the narrative underscores the profound connections we can cultivate with the cosmos and Earth's timeless wonders through eco-holistic practices, urging us to transcend the mundane and touch the infinite.

Chapter 7:

How does nature's embrace, through eco-holistic health, offer solace and strength to our aging hearts yearning for serenity?

Maibong was a small and remote village that rested on the edge of the Silk Route Whispering Forest. The forest was a vast, dense, ancient woodland that stood proud and towering, untouched by human folly over the centuries. The villagers, who lived simple lives and revered Nature, knew of the forest's secrets, and found solace and strength in a secluded glade deep within the woods.

Ms. Loly was the village historian, a woman of age with silver hair cascading like a waterfall down her back. She had witnessed the passing of time, and her once-vibrant eyes now held stories of the past. She was known for her wisdom and knowledge of the village's history, but she kept one secret close to her heart: the sacred glade in the Whispering Forest.

It wasn't until her 90th birthday, when the villagers gathered around her, that she decided to share her secret. She began, "When my heart first felt the weight of years, I stumbled upon the sacred glade in the Whispering Forest. The clearing was surrounded by tall trees, their boughs intertwined in an eternal embrace. But it wasn't just the beauty of the place; it was alive and breathing."

Ms. Loly described how she felt a connection with the Earth beneath her feet, the chirping of the crickets, the rustling of leaves, and the gentle caress of the wind. "The glade is the heart of eco-holistic health," she explained. "It whispered secrets of herbs and roots, of natural remedies. It showed me that aging is not a burden but a celebration."

She continued, "By adopting the ways of the forest, the holistic remedies, I merged my life with Nature. The herbs rejuvenated my body, the forest melodies soothed my spirit, and the wisdom of the trees fortified my aging heart."

Ms. Loly's story spread, and the elders of Maibong started making pilgrimages to the sacred glade. They began to understand that the embrace of Nature was both physical and profoundly spiritual. The forest listened, healed, and embraced their weary souls, giving them serenity.

As time went on, the villagers realized that they had ignored the timeless wisdom of Nature in seeking modern comforts. The holistic approach of the Whispering Forest rejuvenated them, not just by curing ailments but by reconnecting their spirits to the rhythms of the Earth.

A movement began in Maibong. The young were taught about herbs and ancient remedies. Gardens bloomed, filled with medicinal plants. Children grew up understanding the importance of the trees, the water, the soil, and the air. With respect for and gratitude for Nature, Maibong transformed into a haven of health and well-being.

Decades passed, and her teachings continued even though Ms. Loly left the mortal realm. The village became a beacon, attracting those seeking solace, strength, and serenity. The embrace of Nature through eco-holistic health proved to be the elixir for aging hearts yearning for tranquility.

In the heart of the Whispering Forest, time and Nature danced in a perpetual embrace, proving that even in the face of mortality, the soul could find ageless peace with Nature's touch.

Our lives are like a grand theatrical performance, with the gossamer curtains of our memories swaying gently in the winds of time, revealing a vast auditorium of the past of fleeting moments, heartaches, joys, and silent contemplations. With the weight of yesteryear bearing down on us, we're left with a pulsating question that emerges from the heart's core: How exactly do the sacred tenets of eco-holistic health guide our next act and light up the path of a soul-enriched journey forward?

Greetings, readers! Today, I'm thrilled to discuss something that's close to my heart: eco-holistic health. But before we delve into the science and philosophy, I'd like to connect with you all.

Picture a serene morning when the sky is still dark, and the world is quiet. Imagine a lush forest, teeming with life, enveloped in a gentle mist. Every leaf, every twig, and every petal seem to be holding its breath, waiting for the sun to rise.

In this magical moment of transition between night and day, we discover the true essence of eco-holistic health. Just like that forest, our souls also yearn for the nurturing touch of Nature to brighten up our daily lives.

As we wander through this imaginary forest, let's appreciate the babbling brook that flows through it. Its crystal-clear waters reflect the colors of the awakening sky, and its gentle melody feels like a song from another time. The stream teaches us something crucial: life, at its core, is about rhythm.

Eco-holistic health encourages us to recognize this rhythm and turn our daily routines into a harmonious dance. Every step we take every decision we make should be in perfect harmony with Nature's innate choreography. Imagine if every action we took was in perfect harmony with the world around us.

But let's not forget about the birds. Their beautiful songs fill the forest, reminding us to pause in our busy lives and appreciate life's simple pleasures. Moments to listen, to feel, to appreciate the small things in life, like the fragrance of a flower, the rustle of leaves, or the gentle caress of a breeze.

And then the sun rises, and the forest comes alive in a beautiful dance of light and shadows. This dance, this intricate ballet, encapsulates a question that many of us have asked ourselves: How can eco-holistic health transform our mundane routines into something extraordinary?

The answer is simple yet profound. It lies in the rhythms and harmonies of Nature itself. By grounding ourselves in these rhythms, we can transform every moment into a celebration of life's beautiful complexity.

Eco-holistic health is more than just a fad. It's a philosophy, a way of life that connects our individual well-being with the health of the planet. As we look ahead, let's remember that life is a dance, where every step, every twirl, and every leap can be in harmony with Nature's orchestra.

Let's not be bystanders to Nature's beauty. Let's be active participants, integral pieces of this grand, beautiful puzzle. Let's remember that even in the busiest moments of our lives, there is poetry waiting to be discovered.

Thank you all for joining me on this journey today. Let's make eco-holistic health not just a part of our lives but a part of our hearts.

Whispers of Tomorrow: Nature's Lullaby for the Soul

In the village of Sundara, the people believed that at dawn, if one listened with genuine intent, they could hear the Earth's whispers. They said it was Nature's way of nurturing the soul, preparing it for the day ahead.

Maaya, a young woman from Sundara, had often heard tales of these whispers from her grandmother. "The world sings, child," the old woman would say, her eyes distant and her voice soft. "But to hear it, one must not only listen with their ears but also their hearts."

For years, Maaya tried. She'd wake before the village, venturing into the meadows to capture the elusive song. But she was met only with silence.

One morning, following a particularly challenging day, Maaya found herself in the heart of the woods, tears clouding her vision. She felt detached, like a leaf separated from its branch, drifting aimlessly in the vast expanse of life. She was losing hope in the tales of her grandmother. Could it be just another fable?

She sat beneath an ancient oak, its gnarled branches stretching like arms embracing the heavens. And as she closed her eyes, trying to stifle her tears, she felt a gentle breeze. It was like the softest touch—a comforting caress.

And then it began. A quiet hum, so soft it was almost imperceptible. It grew, harmonizing with the rustling leaves, the chirping crickets, and the distant call of a nightingale.

She felt the ground beneath her pulse with life, and every tree, stone, and creature seemed to join this magnificent symphony. The whispers enveloped her, tugging at her heartstrings, weaving a art of hope, love, and resilience.

The whispers spoke of days gone by, of hardships and victories. They talked of tomorrow and the endless possibilities that awaited. They hummed the lullaby of life, a tune that spoke of the interconnectedness of all things.

As dawn broke, Maaya returned to Sundara with tears of joy. She couldn't wait to share her experience. But as she recounted her tale, she realized that words couldn't capture the magic.

The whispers of tomorrow, she realized, were not just an external melody but a reflection of the song within one's soul. It wasn't something to be heard but felt. It was the universe's way of reminding every heart of its inherent strength, beauty, and purpose.

From that day on, Maaya no longer ventured out seeking the whispers. Instead, she'd close her eyes every morning, take a deep breath, and tune into the lullaby that played within her soul. And every so often, when someone in Sundara felt lost or despondent, she'd gently remind them, "Listen, not with your ears but with your heart. For the whispers of tomorrow are Nature's lullaby for the soul."

As we take each step into the enchanted forest, it is as if we are entering a world of infinite possibilities and endless secrets. The ancient trees surrounding us, with their gnarled roots stretching deep within the Earth and their branches that seem to touch the sky above, create a magnificent cathedral where every ray of sunlight is a brushstroke from Nature's palette. It is as if we have been transported to a different realm, where the beauty of personality reigns supreme, and the universe's wonders are waiting to be explored.

The principles of eco-holistic health, which aid us in comprehending and embracing the natural world around us, serve as our guides as we explore this sanctuary. We learn to appreciate the intricate balance of Nature and how everything is interconnected—every tree, every rock, every insect, and every animal.

In a remote glen, a solitary stone stands amidst a sea of lush ferns, and fireflies begin their nocturnal ballet. Despite its age, the rock radiates visible energy. We are transported to a different time and place as we touch its smooth surface. We hear stories of ancient civilizations that revered the wisdom of the Earth and of wise men and women who understood the melodies of the wind and the rhythms of the sea. Here, we are reminded of the ancient practices that have been lost to time—herbal remedies brewed under the light of the full moon, meditative dances around roaring fires, and chants that evoke the spirits of the land.

Although these practices seem forgotten in the modern world, they are vital to transforming our existence. Amid the hustle and bustle of everyday life, these age-old rituals call us to pause, listen, and reconnect with the natural world. By integrating these practices into our daily lives, we give even our most mundane tasks a sense of purpose and find ourselves more in tune with the universe's grand orchestration.

Further ahead, a gentle waterfall cascades from a cliff and its droplets shimmer like diamonds in the sun. This waterfall serves as a reminder of the continuous flow of life—a cycle of birth, growth, decay, and rebirth. By immersing ourselves in these waters, we are reborn, shedding the weariness of yesterday and emerging revitalized, ready to craft a harmonious and balanced future.

But it's not just about the grand moments. The embrace of eco-holistic health also lies in the nuances—in the flutter of a butterfly's wing, the intricate pattern of morning dew on a spider's web, or the soft hum of bees collecting nectar. In these fleeting moments, we are reminded of life's fragile beauty, urging us to cherish each breath, heartbeat, and passing second.

In conclusion, the teachings of eco-holistic health illuminate our path to a transformed future. As we integrate the wisdom of Nature into our daily existence, we don't just exist; we thrive. We become dancers in the grand ballet of life, moving with grace, passion, and an unyielding connection to the world around us. As we continue our journey through the enchanted forest, we weave a art of moments as enchanting as the forest itself.

Key Takeaways from the Text:

· **The Whispering Forest's Significance:** The Silk Route Whispering Forest near Maibong village holds ancient secrets revered by the villagers. The forest remains untouched by human intervention, showcasing its pristine state over the centuries.

· **Ms. Loly's Role:** As the village historian, Ms. Loly carries the wisdom of the village's past. She held a cherished secret about a sacred glade within the Whispering Forest, which she discovered in her younger years. The glade was a source of holistic health, wisdom, and rejuvenation for her.

· **Revelation of the Glade:** Ms. Loly chose to unveil her secret on her 90th birthday. The glade wasn't just a place of beauty. Still, it was a source of spiritual connection and well-being, emphasizing that aging is a celebration rather than a burden.

· **Impact on Villagers**: After learning about the glade, the elders started visiting it and embracing the natural and spiritual healing it provided. The village created a movement for eco-holistic health, teaching younger generations about the importance of Nature, herbs, and ancient remedies.

· **Maibong's Transformation:** As a result of Ms. Loly's teachings and the villagers' newfound respect for Nature, Maibong underwent a significant transformation. They cultivated gardens with medicinal plants, and the village blossomed into a sanctuary of health and well-being.

· **Legacy of Ms. Loly:** Even after Ms. Loly departed from the world, her teachings continued influencing the villagers, turning Maibong into a beacon for seekers of solace and serenity.

· **Metaphorical Reflection:** The forest represents life's mysteries and the endless dance of time and Nature. The embrace of eco-holistic health is about connecting with these natural rhythms and finding ageless peace.

· **The Enchanted Forest Experience:** The story emphasizes the beauty of Nature, from the whispering trees to the gentle waterfalls. It underscores the importance of pausing, reflecting, and reconnecting with the environment around us.

· **The Village of Sundara's Belief:** In another tale, the villagers of Sundara believed in the Earth's whispers at dawn. Maaya's story in this village emphasizes the need to listen with our ears and hearts.

· **Eco-holistic Health in Daily Life:** Integrating Nature's wisdom into daily routines can transform mundane tasks into profound experiences, aligning us with the universe's rhythms.

Additional Questions for Exploration:

· **Herbs and Remedies:** What were the specific natural remedies and herbs that the villagers from Maibong learned from the glade in the Whispering Forest? How were they used to heal and rejuvenate?

· **Ans:** The glade is home to a variety of herbs, each with its own unique properties. The villagers are well-versed in using these herbs, which have been integral to Ayurvedic medicine for generations.

· While the vast majority of these herbs are incredibly beneficial, there is one that requires special attention to avoid any potential risks. The villagers deeply respect these resources and understand the importance of using them mindfully.

· **Ms. Loly's Discovery:** How did Ms. Loly initially stumble upon the sacred glade within the Whispering Forest? What circumstances or events led her there, and why did she keep this profound Discovery a secret for such a long period?

· **Ans:** As per the legend, the people of Bharat had lost touch with the invaluable benefits of Ayurveda, a holistic lifestyle. However, Ms. Loly, a woman with an independent spirit, always sought refuge from the chaos of the modern world. She was aware of the sanctity and beauty of the place. Still, she feared that its balance might be disrupted by the hordes of people who might flock to it once its existence became common knowledge. Her concern for preserving the enchanted space was a testament to her constructive and thoughtful Nature.

· **3. Maibong's Holistic** Transformation: How did the teachings from the glade and adopting eco-holistic health reshape the village's daily routines, cultural practices, and overall ethos? How did it improve both the physical and spiritual health of the villagers?

· **Ans:** Bharat's Ayush promotion is an inspiring example of the positive impact of embracing our natural roots and remedies. The transformation of Maibong is a testament to the power of this approach. For those interested in learning more, an abundance of information is waiting to be discovered.

Chapter 8:

As the sun sets on past chapters and dawns on new beginnings, how can eco-holistic approaches light our path towards holistic wellness?

Eco-holistic approaches light our path towards holistic wellness.

In a peaceful corner of the Silk Route lies a small village called Aleria. Beautiful rolling hills and green fields surround it. In the evening, the villagers gather on the mountain to watch the sunset, like a beautiful painting of oranges, pinks, and purples.

One evening, the village elder, Amarin, shared a story about how their village had learned to live in harmony with nature. She explained that they used eco-friendly ways to care for the land, like using natural methods to help the soil grow healthy again and collecting rainwater instead of taking too much from the Earth. They also planted trees to protect the village from solid winds. They built their homes using natural materials like mud, straw, and stone.

Aleria's methods are unique because they stem from an age-old belief that everything is connected. When I stepped into the village, it was apparent that this was not just a belief but a lifestyle. One of the most memorable things I noticed was their communal gardens. Instead of every family having their own small plot, they all contribute to one massive playground. This not only conserves space but also fosters a sense of community. They're also big on composting, turning all their organic waste into nutritious garden soil. This cycle of giving back to the land is deeply ingrained in their daily lives. Another thing that struck me was how they creatively used rainwater. They had a series of interconnected barrels, channels, and even rooftop gardens, which helped conserve water. The village is like a living, breathing entity, with every home and person playing a part in its well-being.

But it wasn't just about taking care of the land - they also cared for themselves. They practiced meditation and ate healthy food that made them feel physically and mentally sound. Amarin explained that they believed everything was connected and that by taking care of the Earth, they were also taking care of themselves.

The villagers watched the sunset daily as a promise of hope and a new beginning. They believed that living in harmony with nature could create a brighter future for themselves and the planet. This peaceful village shows us that respecting and caring for nature can make a world of hope, beauty, and harmony.

In the grand art of time, the sun gracefully lowers its golden curtain on chapters that have once been, casting a rich, amber glow on the memories etched in its fleeting light. Each sunset, with its vibrant art of reds, oranges, and purples, is not just an ending but a herald of the mysteries that await the promise of a new dawn.

As nature's rhythms move in harmonious cycles of endings and beginnings, we must evolve our understanding of wellness. As the first light of dawn delicately breaks the horizon, it illuminates a path less traveled—that of eco-holistic approaches. This path is a trail and a symbiotic dance between us and the environment. The morning mist reveals the intertwined roots of trees, which mirror our body, mind, and spirit connectedness. The chirping birds sing a song of balance, emphasizing that our well-being is intrinsically tied to the health of the world around us.

In this new chapter, the shimmering dew on leaves reflects the pristine clarity of an eco-holistic approach to wellness. Like the delicate web of a spider glistening in morning's first light, this approach understands that each strand of well-being is connected, from the foods we consume to the air we breathe and the thoughts we nurture. Our health does not exist in isolation but thrives in the rich ecosystem of holistic well-being, particularly nestled high in the mountains, that I'll never forget. Freshly baked bread and blooming jasmine would waft into my tiny guest room every morning. As I wandered the cobbled streets, the soft squelch of muddy pathways would greet my bare feet while children ran past, their laughter echoing. During lunch, I'd often be invited into a local's home.

The taste of their stew, a combination of tangy, spicy, and a hint of sweetness, was like a symphony of flavors that danced on my tongue.
So, as we stand at the crossroads of past and future, let the luminous rays of eco-holistic wisdom guide us. Let them be the lantern that casts a gentle glow on our journey, revealing the delicate balance of nature and the profound interconnectedness of all life. In this harmony,

we find not just wellness but a symphony of holistic vitality that resonates with the very heartbeat of the Earth.

Beneath the vast expanse of the cosmos, where stars twinkle as ancient sentinels of time, our world spins in a dance of perpetual transformation. With its radiant embrace, the setting sun softly whispers tales of days gone by, casting long shadows that blend past wisdom with future hopes.

Each leaf that rustles in the evening breeze carries stories of countless sunrises and sunsets, seasons changing, and life evolving. The profound truths of eco-holistic wellness reside within these whispered tales and the silent rhythms of nature.

Venture deeper into the forest's heart, where the verdant canopy filters the sun's rays into a dappled dance of light and shade. Here, ancient trees stand as guardians of time, their gnarled roots delving deep into the Earth, drawing nourishment from its depths, just as we must seek sustenance for our souls. Every rustling leaf, every chirping cricket, every gentle stream carries a message: to heal oneself is to heal the world. For in the symphony of nature, every note, every rhythm, every pause contributes to the beautiful melody of holistic well-being.

The path ahead, bathed in the moon's soft glow, beckons with the allure of mysteries yet to unfold. As the silvery moonlight filters through the dancing leaves, it casts patterns on the forest floor, each unique yet interconnected. This is the essence of eco-holistic wellness. It teaches us to see not just the individual but the vast web of life in which each being plays a pivotal role.

With each step forward, let the murmurs of the wind and the songs of the night creatures become our guiding anthem. Let the fragrant bloom of flowers and the refreshing kiss of dew on our skin constantly remind us that in seeking wellness, we must embrace both the seen and the unseen, the tangible and the ethereal.

For in the embrace of nature, in the gentle lullaby of rustling leaves and babbling brooks, lies the roadmap to holistic wellness—a journey where every sunset's end is but the precursor to a brighter, more enlightened dawn.
To adopt an eco-holistic lifestyle, there are a few actionable steps we can take. One approach is to prioritize supporting local farmers and artisans by consuming locally sourced food and purchasing local products. This simple shift can have a significant impact on reducing our carbon footprint. Even living in a small space, you can still adopt sustainable practices such as composting and diverting waste from landfills.

Remembering that a holistic approach encompasses more than just the environment is essential. It also includes our overall wellness. Make time for self-care, connect with nature, meditate, or enjoy leisurely walks. Every choice we make, no matter how small, impacts our larger ecosystem.
Drawing from that, here's a deeper exploration into eco-holistic approaches that the villagers in your story might adopt:

Water Harvesting: Villagers could design rooftops and pathways to collect rainwater instead of relying on inconsistent water supplies. They could then filter collected water using sand and charcoal, providing a sustainable water source.

Natural Building Materials: Homes built using mud, straw, and bamboo are not only eco-friendly but also offer natural insulation, keeping interiors cool during summers and warm during winters.

Companion Planting: The villagers could practice companion planting, where certain plants are grown together to deter pests, improve growth, or enhance flavor. For example, beans, corn, and squash – known as the "Three Sisters" – support and benefit from each other when planted together, just like Jai's marigolds.

Community Composting: All organic waste could be collected and converted into rich compost, returning nutrients to the soil and reducing waste.

Solar and Wind Energy: The villagers could harness the sun's and wind's power, using handmade windmills and rudimentary solar panels for their minimal energy needs.

If you're interested in exploring such sustainable practices further, "The One-Straw Revolution" by Masanobu Fukuoka is a fabulous read. It's a deep dive into natural farming and the philosophy of working with nature rather than against it. Websites like PermacultureNews.org are treasure troves of real-life examples and practical solutions. Joining local permaculture groups or attending workshops can provide hands-on experience and insights.

The beauty of eco-holistic living is its simplicity and profound respect for nature. As the story unfolds, let the readers feel the breeze, taste the freshness of naturally grown foods, and marvel at the ingenious solutions of the villagers. It's a journey worth exploring. Happy writing and eco-exploring!

When Sunsets Illuminate Pathways to Wellness

First off, what a beautifully worded question! "When Sunsets Illuminate Pathways to Wellness" instantly evoked some cherished memories from my past. As I mentioned in my introduction, I was going through a rough patch as a teenager. My days seemed monotonous, and I felt disconnected from the world. One evening, I was at a beach, watching the sunset. How the orange hues danced over the water got me thinking: What if this moment of tranquility could be a metaphor for my journey to wellness? It reminded me that there's beauty at the end of every day, no matter how tough it is. This sunset became a pivot for me. Every evening, no matter where I was, I'd take a moment to watch the sun go down, reflecting on my day, my feelings, and myself. This daily ritual brought a sense of calmness and reflection that played a massive role in my overall well-being.

As for some practical tips, here they are:
Allow me to share some tips to help you discover peace, motivation, and personal development in your daily life:

· **1. The Wisdom of Nature:** Nature provides many ways to heal and uplift us. Consider taking a stroll in the park, stargazing, or listening to the sound of waves to discover your "sunset moment." Make it a daily habit to connect with nature.

· **2. Mindful Meditation:** Combine your sunset watching with mindfulness meditation. Begin with just five minutes daily, focusing on your breath, sensations, or the beauty in front of you.

· **3. Journaling**: Documenting your thoughts, reflections, and emotions can assist you in gaining a better understanding of yourself and tracking your emotional growth.

· **4. Community:** Seek out a community of individuals who share your interests and passions. Whether chasing sunsets or something else entirely, being part of a community can allow you to share your stories experiences and grow together.

If you're keen to delve deeper, I'd recommend the book "The Nature Fix" by Florence Williams. It beautifully illustrates the relationship between nature and our well-being.

Remember, the journey to wellness is personal, ever evolving, and, most importantly, worth every moment of effort. Dive deep, explore, and let those sunsets illuminate your path. Cheers!

As we gaze into the infinite expanse of the universe, we are reminded of our fragile existence. Our planet is a tiny blue dot floating amidst the vast cosmic ballet of galaxies and black holes. But the sunset holds a profound significance beyond its astronomical phenomenon within this grand celestial theater.

As the sun descends below the horizon, the sky transforms into a canvas of reds and gold, and the world is enveloped in a symphonic adieu to the known, beckoning us toward endless possibilities. The sunset resonates with the deepest chords of our soul, offering us a glimpse of the infinite beyond. It is a portal that leads us to the profundities of the cosmos and, by extension, to the essence of our existence.

The stars shimmer above as night falls, and the gentle breeze whispers ancient secrets. The nocturnal wind speaks of the age-old dance between the macrocosm and the microcosm, as the universe mirrors the intricate neural pathways of our minds. The infinite expanse of interstellar space echoes the boundless depths of our consciousness. In the forest, moonbeams play hide and seek amidst the foliage, carrying the wisdom of eons.

To understand the eco-holistic journey toward wellness is to embrace the interconnectedness of all things. It is to realize that we are stardust and dreams woven into the art of existence. This journey is not just about integrating our body, mind, and spirit with nature's rhythms. It is an odyssey into the essence of being, an exploration of the unseen dimensions that interlace every atom, thought, and emotion.

The murmuring streams carry tales of mountain springs and the cosmic rivers that flow through the fabric of spacetime itself. To tread this path of eco-holistic enlightenment is to embrace the cosmic dance of balance and harmony. It is an ever-evolving journey that teaches us that true wellness is not a destination but a way of life.

As we dive deeper into the night, let the constellations guide us. Within their stellar patterns lies the ancient knowledge that holistic wellness is not just about the convergence of body, mind, and spirit but the alignment of the self with the infinite. It is the melding of the mortal with the eternal, a journey that brings us closer to the very essence of existence itself.

The article highlights several key takeaways:

1. **Aleria's Tranquility:** Aleria is a serene village along the Silk Route, surrounded by breathtaking scenery. Its colorful sunsets, lush green fields, and rolling hills make it a picturesque location.

1. **Harmonious Living:** The villagers adhere to an eco-friendly lifestyle rooted in their belief in the interconnectedness of all things. This philosophy is integrated into their daily routines.

1. **Sustainable Practices:** The village has implemented various eco-friendly measures, such as constructing homes with natural materials like mud, straw, and stone and maintaining communal gardens.

1. **Water Conservation**: Aleria's innovative rainwater harvesting system, consisting of interconnected barrels, channels, and rooftop gardens, is a notable feature of the village.

1. **Holistic Wellness:** The villagers prioritize holistic wellness by practicing meditation, consuming healthy foods, and nurturing nature, which they believe equates to self-care.

1. **Eco-holistic Approaches:** The article emphasizes the importance of adopting an eco-holistic lifestyle, such as supporting local artisans, composting, and regular self-care.

1. **Sunsets as Metaphors:** Sunsets in Algeria represent hope, endings, and new beginnings, reminding villagers of the cycles of life and the promise of a brighter future.

1. **Wellness is Interconnected:** The article emphasizes that well-being is closely linked to the environment, and the planet's and its inhabitants' well-being is inextricably intertwined.

1. **Universe and Wellness:** Recognizing the interconnectedness of all things, including the cosmos and natural patterns, is the key to genuine health and wellness.

1. **Deep Resonance with Nature:** By appreciating the rhythms of nature, such as rustling leaves and babbling brooks, we can discover a roadmap to holistic wellness. Embracing these rhythms is the key to a well-rounded, healthy life.

Overall, the article presents a compelling case for living in harmony with the environment by intertwining the themes of nature, sustainability, and holistic well-being.

Chapter 9:

What timeless lessons from the earth can help us age gracefully, embracing each moment with gratitude and grace?

The Parable of the Ancient Tree

In the center of India, an inspiring story has been told for centuries - a tale of finding enlightenment under the shade of an old tree. The Mahabodhi, a symbol of knowledge and age, has silently observed the world transform, offering shelter to Buddha Goya as he attained enlightenment and spreading serenity to anyone who sought refuge under its shade. But like every story, the legend of Mahabodhi is not just about a tree; it's about comprehending, having patience, and the significant connections of life.

I embarked on a journey to witness the Mahabodhi, to see its magnificence, and to understand the parable it represented. As I neared the sacred city of Bodh Gaya, the atmosphere seemed to whisper tales of wise men and divine meetings. The horizon painted a picture of the sun rising behind numerous stupas and ancient monasteries, each containing countless more stories of enlightenment.

Entering the Mahabodhi Temple Complex, my attention was immediately drawn to the majestic ancient tree. There, surrounded by devotees and monks, stood the Mahabodhi—the tree under which Siddhartha Gautama, also known as Buddha, found enlightenment.

An elderly monk, sensing my admiration, walked over and began sharing the story of the ancient tree. "In a time long ago, a young prince, disenchanted with the sufferings of life, sat beneath this very tree, vowing not to leave until he found the truth. Days turned into weeks. With unwavering determination, he meditated. And one day, as the first light of dawn broke, Siddhartha became the Buddha, having uncovered the truth of life."

I sat down, hoping to grasp this tree's lessons. The monk continued, "Much like the Buddha, this tree has endured. It remains through storms, droughts, and the ravages of time, teaching us perseverance."

"But the real lesson," the monk whispered, "is not about perseverance. It's about interconnection. Look at those leaves?" He pointed upward. "Each one is nurtured by the same roots, yet each is unique. So, too, are we. Our roots - our experiences, memories, and ancestors—shape us. Yet, each of us is a unique leaf, playing a singular role in the vast tapestry of existence."

The Mahabodhi is more than an ancient tree. It's a reminder of the passage of time, a witness to the profound journey of a prince-turned-Buddha, and a parable of our interconnected existence.

As I left Bodh Gaya, the image of the tree was engraved in my heart, reminding me constantly of the timeless tales and wisdom it quietly conveys.

> undefined The Mahabodhi is an ancient tree in India, under which Buddha found enlightenment.

undefined It is a symbol of knowledge, age, and interconnectedness.
undefined The tree has endured through time, teaching us about perseverance and interconnection.
undefined Our planet is a testament to the passage of time and the beauty that comes with it
undefined Nature teaches us valuable lessons, such as resilience, acceptance, letting go, and gratitude.

Hello and welcome, readers. Let's talk about something so evident yet so often overlooked— the timeless beauty of our planet.

When we look up at our blue skies, what do we see? It's not just an expanse of color. It's a canvas of stories and legacies from the past. Think about our magnificent mountains or the deep mysteries of our oceans. They aren't just geographical landmarks or water bodies. They're poems written over time, showing us how age can add layers of beauty.

How many of us are morning people here? Even if you're not, think about the sunrise. That moment when the sky transforms from a murky blue to a vibrant canvas of oranges, pinks, and golds. It's not just a daily phenomenon; it's a powerful reminder. Each dawn brings with it the promise of new beginnings, new dreams, and new passions. The sun, in its radiant glory, challenges the darkness and invites us to do the same in our lives.

Now, imagine a tree. Tall, majestic. Its branches strive upwards while its roots delve deep into the Earth. There's a quiet strength in that image, isn't there? Trees symbolize resilience and growth despite adversities. And aren't we all like trees? The lines on our skin, much like tree rings, narrate tales of our challenges, our triumphs, and the lessons we've embraced.

And then there's the ocean. How many of us feel calm just listening to the sound of waves? There's a lesson in their rhythmic dance. The ebb and flow teach us to move gracefully with time, to accept changes as they come, and to understand that just like tides, moments of high and low are part and parcel of our journey.

Ah, autumn. It's a season of crisp air and colors that look like they've been borrowed from an artist's palette. Those red, gold, and amber leaves? They're not just nature's decor. They remind us of the elegance of letting go. As we grow older, like those leaves, we learn the art of cherishing what adds value and gently releasing what doesn't.

But, amidst all these lessons, there's one that stands out the most: Gratitude. Our Earth, in all its vastness, is a living testament to thankfulness. From a tiny bloom to the mighty mountain ranges, everything whispers words of appreciation. Our experiences, our memories, and our shared love are all threads in the tapestry of life. And isn't it magnificent?

Let's not merely exist. Let's resonate with the symphony of our Earth, adding our own notes of joy, gratitude, and love. Let's make each day, each moment, a heartfelt exchange.

Thank you for sharing this moment with me today. Let's keep exchanging beauty, love, and gratitude with our Earth and with each other.

Embracing Earth's Timeless Whispers

Embracing Earth's Timeless Whispers: A Journey to the Pyramids

The sun hung like an amber pendant in the Egyptian sky, its warm hues kissing the colossal structures of the ancient pyramids of Giza. Standing at the base, one can't help but be overwhelmed by their magnificence and the mysteries they've held for millennia. I had embarked on this journey to embrace the timeless whispers of the Earth, and where else to start but where time seems to have paused to pay homage?

The legends of the pharaohs, their vast kingdoms, and the mysteries hidden within these pyramids have always fascinated me. But being there, in that moment, surrounded by the raw energy of these ancient marvels, was unlike anything any book or documentary could ever portray. The pyramids weren't just enormous stone structures; they were stories, memories, and a testament to the brilliance and ambition of a civilization long gone.

I entered the Pyramid of Khufu, the largest pyramid, under the guidance of an elderly local named Hasim. The narrow passageways and chambers inside starkly contrasted with the vastness outside. The inscribed hieroglyphic walls seemed to come alive, revealing tales of valor, love, and devotion to the deities. With his deep-set eyes and weathered face, Hasim narrated stories passed down through generations, each intertwined with the next, much like the threads of a tapestry.

"The Earth here," Hasim whispered, placing his hand flat on the cold stone floor of the King's Chamber, "has seen the rise and fall of pharaohs, the love stories of queens, the ambitions of builders, and the hopes of every soul that tread this land."

That evening, as we emerged from the pyramid and the desert air greeted us with a gentle, cool embrace, I sat down on the golden sands, gazing at the enigmatic structures illuminated by the sun. The horizon was painted with orange, pink, and purple shades, and the pyramids cast long, dark shadows that seemed to merge with the approaching night.

I closed my eyes briefly, and it was as if I could hear the Earth's whispers. These were the secrets of the sands, tales of courage, stories of entire lifetimes, and the dreams of a civilization that once was.

My journey to the pyramids wasn't just a trip to an archaeological site. It was a profound, soul-stirring experience, connecting me to the timeless rhythms of the Earth, its ageless wisdom, and its eternal stories.

Today, as I pen down this experience, I feel a deep connection with all those who walked the Earth before us. Embracing the Earth's timeless whispers has taught me that we are but a small chapter in the vast saga of our planet. As we write our own stories, we should do so with love, respect, and an understanding that they will someday become whispers for future generations to cherish and learn from.

Nestled beneath the vast azure skies, our Earth has been an enduring sentinel of time, whispering tales of eons gone by. Its undulating landscapes, from the rugged, age-old mountains to the deep, mysterious oceans, hold within their embrace lessons on aging with unparalleled elegance. To journey through life, drawing from Earth's ancient wisdom, is to gracefully embrace the art of aging.

As the golden sun slowly inches across the horizon, casting its first rosy blush over the world, it reminds us of the "beauty of beginnings." Even as we age, each day brings forth a fresh canvas of possibilities. Just as the dawn breaks through the darkness, we, too, can light up our later years with renewed dreams and passions.

With their gnarled branches reaching for the heavens and roots delving deep into the soil, the mighty trees speak of "resilience." They have withstood the test of time and weathered countless storms yet stand tall and magnificent. Similarly, as the years etch lines onto our faces, they are testimonies of the battles we've fought, the laughter we've shared, and the wisdom we've gained. To age gracefully is to wear these lines as badges of honor, testaments to a life well-lived.

With their rhythmic dance of ebb and flow, Oceans teaches us about "acceptance." Just as the tides graciously accept their constant change, moving in and out with poise, we, too, can learn to welcome the shifts that age brings. Instead of resisting the natural progression of life, we can dance in harmony with its ebbs and flows.

And as the leaves, in their vibrant hues of reds, golds, and oranges, let go during the autumn, they narrate the beauty of "letting go." With time, we gather experiences, memories, and sometimes, baggage. Aging gracefully requires the wisdom to discern what to hold onto and what to release, allowing ourselves to be as weightless and free as a falling leaf.

But perhaps the most poignant lesson is that of "gratitude." From the blooming petals that unfurl to greet the morning light to the silent mountains that stand sentinel under the starry nights, the Earth sings a song of thankfulness. As we tread this journey of life, every wrinkle, every gray hair, and every memory is a reason to be grateful. For in them lies the essence of our existence, the stories we've lived, and the love we've shared.

To age gracefully, drawing inspiration from the timeless Earth is to move through the tapestry of time with gratitude and grace. It is to honor every scar and celebrate every laugh line, understanding that they are but chapters in life's beautiful, ever-unfolding story.

Let's consider for a moment our magnificent Earth, a storybook older than the most ancient myths whispered in hushed reverence. Through its grand narrative, our planet eloquently weaves tales that leave us spellbound. Its timeless symphony carries harmonies that sing stories of epochs, providing insights into the art of graceful aging, as ageless as the cosmos themselves.

Envision, if you can, the magic of twilight. That ephemeral instant when the day's last light meets the night's first embrace. In that tender pause, the world seems to catch its breath, awaiting the night's whispered secrets. This sublime interlude teaches us that aging isn't about the fading of a day but the beckoning of a star-filled night. It suggests that life's true essence resides not in milestones achieved but in the transitions between them.

Now, cast your gaze on the towering mountains. Monuments that have seen eons come and go, with summits caressing the skies and roots anchored in Earth's core. They're the embodiment of resilience and perspective . Time, rather than diminishing them, has only heightened their majesty. They urge us to perceive aging as an evolution, where each passing year carves us into a more magnificent version of ourselves.

The boundless oceans, with depths we're yet to fathom, tell stories older than humanity. Their rhythmic dance with shores, a delicate interplay of give and take , teaches us life's ebb and flow. They intimate that aging is a dance, a graceful oscillation between releasing the old and welcoming the new.

Have you ever stilled yourself in an ancient woodland, listening intently? If so, you'd realize trees communicate in lifetimes. Their concentric rings aren't mere markers of age, but chronicles of challenges overcome, and joys embraced. They exemplify the beauty of quiet growth , where each silently passed year enriches our soul.

Then, there's the cosmos—an endless expanse where stars are mere pinpricks. It offers a humbling perspective on the grandiosity of our fleeting existence. Amidst the cosmic theater, our lifespans are but a heartbeat. Yet, each joy, sorrow, and memory contribute to the universe's intricate ballet. In this grand context, aging is less about decline and more about deepening our essence within eternity's vast tapestry.

In Earth's gentle hold, we unearth a revelation: aging isn't merely a passage of time. It's a journey into depth, wisdom, and significance. It's a call to cherish every tick of the clock with gratitude, understanding that every moment in the cosmic dance is an ode to the intricate, beautiful weave of existence."

Key takeaways from the content provided:

1. The Mahabodhi Legacy: An ancient tree located in India, the Mahabodhi witnessed Buddha's enlightenment. It stands as a symbol of knowledge, age, endurance, and the intricate web of life's interconnections.

1. Nature's Timeless Lessons: From the vast landscapes to the daily sunrise, our planet's beauty offers insights into resilience, acceptance, the art of letting go, and the importance of gratitude in our daily lives.

1. The Earth as a Storyteller: Our planet isn't just a collection of natural phenomena; it's a narrator of tales that span ages, teaching us about aging with grace and embracing the essence of our existence.

1. The Beauty of Beginnings: Each dawn brings a promise of new beginnings, reminding us that even as we age, every day is an opportunity for renewal and new experiences.

1. Trees as Metaphors: Trees, with their deep roots and expansive branches, embody resilience and growth amidst adversities. Like trees, humans too can stand tall, embracing the challenges and triumphs that come with age.

1. Ocean's Dance of Acceptance: The ebb and flow of the ocean show us the beauty of embracing life's changes. Aging, like the tides, has its highs and lows, but each phase can be embraced gracefully.

1. The Pyramids' Timeless Whispers: The ancient pyramids of Egypt, with their stories of pharaohs, love, and ambition, connect us to Earth's ageless

wisdom and remind us of our transient role in the grand timeline of existence.

1. Embracing Transitions: As day transitions into night during twilight, it reveals that aging is not about the end of an era but the beginning of another. Transitions, whether in life or age, are opportunities for growth and reflection.

1. Mountains' Resilience: Towering mountains, having witnessed countless eons, teach us about the grandeur that comes with resilience and perspective. Time enhances their beauty, just as it can with our aging selves.

1. Cosmic Perspective: When viewed against the backdrop of the vast cosmos, our lives are fleeting. However, every experience, emotion, and memory play a crucial role in the intricate dance of existence. Aging is an opportunity to deepen our understanding and appreciate our place in the universe.

These takeaways encapsulate the wisdom and beauty of the Earth and its teachings on aging gracefully and embracing every moment of our existence.

Chapter 10:

How can the symphony of the natural world bring healing harmony to the challenges faced in our golden age?

Whispers of the Wind: A Symphony of Healing

Elena was alone, sitting on her veranda, looking at the distant horizon. The sky was blue, and the sun was setting, casting golden hues across the landscape. In the past, she was surrounded by the hum of technology, but now she chooses to be alone with nature.

In front of her, a green meadow rustled with life. Wildflowers danced gracefully, creating a soft chorus of whispers. Each bloom represented a vibrant note, a testament to nature's enduring symphony. The colors of the flowers – deep purples, fiery reds, and gentle pinks – painted a visual orchestra that entranced the senses.

In the distance, an ancient oak tree stood majestically. Its gnarled branches swayed; beckoning Elena closer. She often marveled at its strength, how it had weathered countless storms yet continued to thrive, drawing sustenance from the Earth, and standing tall.

Elena reflected on the challenges of her era. The "golden age" was full of advancements but also dilemmas. The rapid pace of change had left many feeling unmoored, longing for a touchstone to ground them.

She closed her eyes and listened to the gentle murmurs of the world around her. A brook babbled nearby, its clear waters carrying tales of ancient times and forgotten secrets. Birds sang from their perches, melodies of hope and joy that stitched together the art of life. Even the wind played its part, caressing leaves and crafting harmonies that soothed the weary soul.

At this moment, she understood nature's symphony's profound healing. By immersing oneself in nature, one could find a balm for the soul, a remedy for the discordant notes that occasionally marred the music of life. The symphony of the natural world, in all its splendor, provided a healing harmony that resonated with the heart, mending its fractures, and restoring its vigor.

Days turned into weeks, and Elena's veranda became a sanctuary for many. People from all walks of life visited, seeking the therapeutic embrace of the wild. They listened, reflected, and healed, finding solace in the timeless melodies the world generously offered.

Ultimately, the ageless symphony of nature provided a compass to guide humanity toward harmony, unity, and inner peace. It served as a testament that even in an era of glittering achievements, the most straightforward tunes held the power to heal and inspire.

Have you ever found yourself lost in the beauty of nature, perhaps standing on a mountaintop, and feeling the wind gently brush past your skin? It's a moment of peace, a chance to connect with something greater than us. The wind is a symphony of stories, secrets, and healing, waiting for those willing to listen.

As we explore the mysteries of metaphysics, we often encounter weighty questions about the essence of existence, causality, and truth. But sometimes, the answers we seek are found in the simplest things. The wind constantly connects us to the world, weaving histories, emotions, and dreams together. It reminds us that we are all part of something greater and that there is beauty in the cyclical patterns of nature.

When we think about ethics, we consider the moral fabric of our actions and decisions. The wind touches all without judgment or discrimination. It simply is . In this way, it can be seen as a blueprint for kindness, acceptance, and healing.

The ancient Greeks had a term, "Pneuma," which referred to both 'wind' and 'spirit.' There may be a deeper connection between our spirit and the world around us than we realize.

As with any philosophical contemplation, it's essential to approach with caution. While the wind has historically symbolized change and movement, we cannot definitively prescribe its healing properties. However, through the lenses of various philosophical domains, there is a compelling argument to be made about its therapeutic potential.

So, the next time you feel the wind on your skin, take a moment to pause and listen. There may be whispers, stories, and lessons waiting to be heard. As with many truths in philosophy, sometimes the most profound answers are found in the quiet, subtle moments.

Nature's Deep Resonance in the Age of Gold

I cannot help but express my fascination with "Nature's Deep Resonance in the Age of Gold." The moment I came across it, my mind was immediately transported back to a personal journey I undertook a few years ago.

During my backpacking trip to the Andes, I stumbled upon a remote village where the elders spoke of a time called the "Age of Gold." It was not about the precious metal but instead pertained to an era when people lived in harmony with nature, treasured every sunrise, each whispering wind, and bird chirping as if pure gold. This reminiscence has stayed with me ever since, and I have always felt the disconnect with our modern age. I spent nights under the stars, gathering around a crackling fire with the villagers, sharing stories and traditions from their forefathers. Their tales were not solely about nature but about resonating with life itself.

The critical insight I gained while with these people is that the deep resonance with nature goes beyond appreciating its beauty. Instead, it is about tuning in to its rhythm, cycles, ebb, and flow. A perfect example is how trees shed their leaves in fall and rejuvenate in spring. This lesson teaches us to let go of the old and embrace the new. You should try living in line with nature's clock for a week. Wake up with the sun, indulge in seasonal foods, and take walks to genuinely observe the world around you. You can also delve into books like "The Hidden Life of Trees" by Peter Wohl Leben or "The Nature Fix" by Florence Williams. These are excellent starting points. Additionally, joining communities like "Holistic Lifestyle Tribe" or Facebook groups dedicated to nature meditation can provide valuable shared experiences.

This deep resonance is not just a one-time experience but a journey that will continually reward you with peace, insights, and a rejuvenated soul. I am excited for you to embark on this quest. Nature has a way of whispering secrets to those who listen. So, happy exploring and resonating!

In a time long ago, when humankind was but a whisper in the vastness of the universe, nature was the eternal melody that serenaded every living being. This was a time of great prosperity, where wealth was not measured in material possessions but rather in the richness of one's communion with the world around them. The resonance of nature was profound, deep, and far-reaching, touching every aspect of life and shaping the essence of existence itself.

The trees stood tall and proud, their leaves shimmering in the sun's golden light. The forests were sacred cathedrals, where the choir comprised the birds and beasts that called them home. The rivers flowed with pristine clarity, carrying stories of distant mountains and valleys and touching the lives of all those they encountered.

Every breeze that brushed against the skin was like a whisper from a distant land; every drop of rain carried secrets from the heavens above. The world was alive with a symphony of harmonies, a dance of elements, all interconnected and resonating with a deep, undying song of existence.

At this time, humans were not conquerors but rather humble participants in the grand art of life. They walked softly on the Earth, their voices harmonious with the wind. They understood true wealth was not the lustrous metal they could hold in their hands but the golden moments of connection, understanding, and being one with the world.

Communities thrived around the tenets of coexistence, living in harmony with the terrain rather than against it. Cultures blossomed with stories, myths, and legends that echoed the rhythms of nature. Ceremonies and festivals celebrated the cyclical patterns of the seasons, the moon's mysteries, and the stars' brilliance.

But the external harmony and the internal resonance made this time genuinely golden. Hearts pulsated with gratitude, minds expanded with wonder, and spirits soared with freedom. The boundary between the self and the universe became porous, allowing for a deep exchange of energy, wisdom, and love.

As time evolved, there were inevitable challenges, but the foundation of deep resonance with nature provided resilience. When storms raged, communities held together, drawing strength from the timeless wisdom of the Earth. When droughts tested their resolve, they looked to the skies and found hope in the promise of rain.

In the age of gold, every sunrise was a reminder of the world's beauty, and every sunset was a testament to its impermanence. It was an era where the heartbeat of the cosmos was felt in every rustling leaf, every flowing stream, and every human embrace.

While time may have moved us forward, the echoes of this golden age remain. They remind us that amidst the clamor of modernity, there exists a deeper resonance, a call back to nature, a yearning for a world where gold isn't just a metal but a state of being, a richness of the soul. And using the timeless resonance of nature itself as a guide, we can find our way back to that era.

In the Age of Gold, the deep resonance of nature genuinely shone brightest.

Screens and digital technology rule the world we live in today. As a result, we frequently lose sight of the value of the fundamental things around us. We often overlook the ancient whispers of the world and become engrossed in the digital screams. However, in our quietest moments, we can't help but feel drawn to nature. Our soul inevitably yearns for the primordial embrace of the natural world, seeking the familiar touch of an age-old tree, the gentle murmur of a babbling brook, or the soaring majesty of mountain ranges. These spaces are more than just physical places; they are time archives.

The natural world contains stories of love, loss, triumph, and tragedy that predate and will outlive us. Each strand of moss, each ripple on the water, is a chronicle of eons past, and we must remember this. Mankind's advancements are incredible, and we have the power to reshape the face of the Earth, from crafting vast, digital landscapes to erecting towering cities. However, our souls are older than our technologies, and we carry the legacy of our ancestors. This legacy was crafted not in the digital realm but in the lap of nature.

When modern life feels overwhelming, many instinctively retreat to the woods, the mountains, or the sea. These spaces offer a return to simplicity and a sanctuary from the cacophony of progress. Here, we remember that before we were consumers, employees, or digital entities, we were simply humans - creatures of the Earth.

The natural world has a deep and profound impact on our lives, and there's a reason why the sound of rain is calming, or the sight of a horizon stretching endlessly makes our hearts swell with emotion. These are not just environmental phenomena; they're connections, bridges to a time when humanity was deeply intertwined with the rhythms of the world.

As we stand at the crossroads of humanity's future, facing immense challenges and uncertainties, we must remember that our best answers might not always lie ahead. Sometimes, they reside in the past, in the deep reservoirs of nature's wisdom. We can find guidance and hope by turning our gaze to these reservoirs and respecting and understanding them.

So, let's ensure we keep the melody of the Earth as we continue our dance of progress. We will find our most accurate, harmonious song in this balance between the old and the new, the tangible and the intangible.

Here are the key takeaways from the text provided:

1. Nature: The dominant theme throughout the text, highlighting its beauty, healing power, and the resonance it brings to individuals.

1. Resonance: The deep connection humans can feel with nature, going beyond superficial appreciation and into a profound spiritual relationship.

1. Symphony: Used to describe nature's harmonious sounds and sights, from the rustling leaves to the birds' songs.

1. Harmony: Represents the balance and unity that nature embodies and the ideal state of human society in resonance with the environment.

1. Golden Age: A metaphorical era symbolizing a time of deep connection with nature, a wealth of experiences, and an understanding of the world.

1. Healing: The therapeutic properties of nature, providing solace, mending souls, and offering peace.

1. Technology: Contrasting the digital and natural worlds, emphasizing the importance of balance between progress and preservation.

1. Wisdom: The insights and understanding gained from nature, the stories it tells, and the lessons it offers.

1. Communion: Sharing, connecting, and being in tune with nature and its elements.

1. Legacy: The enduring impact of nature, its timelessness, and the continuity of its influence on humanity across ages.

These keywords encapsulate the passages' essence, emphasizing nature's therapeutic and spiritual qualities, the deep connections humans can foster with the environment, and the contrast between modernity and a more harmonious past.

Conclusion

As we strive towards progress and success, we often overlook the invaluable wisdom that comes with age and experience. The act of embracing our elders is not just a physical gesture but a symbolic representation of accepting and integrating their knowledge, insights, and experiences. In today's fast-paced world, where technology and innovation are driving us forward, it is important to acknowledge that true wisdom is not solely based on acquiring information but on life's experiences. This "elderly embrace" bridges the past and present, offering us valuable insights that can help us overcome the various challenges we encounter. Through my journey, I have realized that while the world is changing at an extraordinary pace, life's lessons remain the same. By embracing the wisdom of our elders, we not only pay homage to their contributions but enrich our lives with timeless guidance. As we move forward, let us not forget to look back and reach for the hands of those who preceded us. Their stories and experiences hold the key to unlocking secrets that can help us navigate through our own lives. To navigate our future with grace, wisdom, and love.

Disclaimer:

Please note the following disclaimer before reading "Outsmarting Elderly Embrace." This book inspires and provides insights based on personal experiences and observations of the authors and is intended for informational purposes only.

Readers are advised to use their judgment and discretion when applying the content to their situations. The authors have made their best effort to ensure the accuracy and completeness of the information provided but make no warranty or guarantee concerning the content's reliability, suitability, or accuracy.

The authors, publishers, and distributors cannot be held responsible for any loss, injury, claim, liability, or damage resulting from the application or misinterpretation of any material presented. If you have specific concerns or situations requiring professional guidance, please consult an appropriate specialist or professional.

Remember, this book serves to inspire and provide a reflective perspective on elderly relationships and should not be taken as a definitive guide. Everyone's experience is unique, and the path to understanding and embracing the elderly journey is deeply personal. Use this book as a tool, and always trust your wisdom to find your way.

Copyright Notice

References related to the themes and topics of elderly relationships, companionship in later life, and the challenges and joys of aging together, here are a few notable books and articles on the subject:

1. Books:

"The 36-Hour Day" by Nancy L. Mace and Peter V. Rabins: A classic resource for caregivers of people with Alzheimer's disease, dementia, and memory loss in later life.

-"The Secret Life of the Grown-up Brain: The Surprising Talents of the Middle-Aged Mind" by Barbara Strauch: A look into how the brain matures and changes as we age.

-"A Man Called Ove" by Fredrik Backman: A novel that deals with the complexities of aging, relationships, and societal roles.

-"The Gift of Years: Growing Older Gracefully" by Joan Chittister: Reflections on the many aspects of aging, its challenges, and its opportunities.

2. Articles:

-"Later-Life Love: Romance and New Relationships in Later Years" from Psychology Today: This article discusses how romantic relationships in later life differ from younger relationships and their unique strengths.

-"Relationships in old age: More than just family and friends" from The Gerontologist: A deep dive into the importance of diverse relationships in elderly life, beyond just familial connections

-"The Science of Senior Sex" from AARP: A detailed look into the intimacy, challenges, and misconceptions surrounding senior relationships.

3. Journals:

-"The Journals of Gerontology" : A series of journals that cover the broad spectrum of the social sciences and humanities in aging.

-"Ageing and Society": An interdisciplinary journal devoted to the understanding of human ageing and the circumstances of older people.

These references provide a mix of academic, practical, and narrative perspectives on the subject. They can offer valuable insights and context to anyone interested in understanding the intricacies of relationships and companionship in the later stages of life.

Dear Valued Reader,

First and foremost, thank you for immersing yourself in "Outsmarting Elderly Embrace." We hope that you found the content enlightening and resonant.

Your feedback is of utmost importance to us. Reviews help future readers determine if this book is right for them and guide us as we continue our journey of sharing meaningful stories and insights with the world.

If you're willing, we'd be immensely grateful if you could take a few minutes to leave a review:

1. Share your connection: Did a particular story or lesson resonate with you? How did the book impact your perspective on elderly relationships?

2. Offer constructive feedback: We continually strive to improve. Any insights or suggestions you have will be invaluable for our future endeavors.

3. Recommend the book: If you believe "Outsmarting Elderly Embrace" could benefit others, please let them know in your review. Leaving a review is simple on Amazon, my website, etc.

Thank you once again for joining us on this journey. Whether filled with praise, constructive criticism, or a mix of both, every review brings value and perspective. We truly appreciate your time and thoughts.

Warm regards,

DADHIRAM BASUMATARY